Close Encounters with Insects and Spiders

Close Encounters
with Insects
and Spiders

WRITTEN AND ILLUSTRATED BY JAMES B. NARDI

Iowa State University Press / Ames

© 1988 Iowa State University Press
All rights reserved

Composed by Iowa State University Press, Ames, Iowa 50010
Printed in the United States of America

First edition, 1988
Second printing, 1990

Library of Congress Cataloging-in-Publication Data

Nardi, James B., 1948–
    Close encounters with insects and spiders / written and illustrated
by James B. Nardi.—1st ed.
        p.   cm.
    Bibliography: p.
    Includes index.
    ISBN 0-8138-1978-4
    1. Insects   2. Spiders.   [1. Insects.   2. Spiders]   I. Title.

QL467.N24   1988   87-26284
595.7—dc19   CIP

James B. Nardi received his B.S. degree from
Purdue University and his Ph.D. degree from Harvard
University. He was a NATO postdoctoral fellow at the
Medical Research Council Laboratory of Molecular
Biology, Cambridge, England, and is now Research
Scientist, Department of Entomology, University of Il-
linois.

CONTENTS

PREFACE

CHILDREN have a natural curiosity and fondness for little creatures, and in this respect, I was no exception. I was one of those children, however, who never quite outgrew the sense of wonder and fascination for little creatures. I was fortunate that my parents never discouraged my curiosity; they graciously welcomed all the insect guests that I brought home.

Growing up on a farm in Indiana was a good introduction to insects and spiders. Their lives proved so fascinating to me that I decided to make a career of studying them.

Even after years of observing and studying insects in the field and in the laboratory, I am constantly surprised and amazed by them. Whether I travel to new places or simply take familiar paths, I continually meet new species and make new discoveries. Drawing the creatures that I view at close range demands careful observation and has enabled me to see features that I probably would otherwise not have noticed. Each individual has an awesome symmetry, even down to the positioning of individual bristles and hairs. These pages share with the readers this rather foreign, but intriguing, perspective on the world of insects and spiders that I have been so fortunate to enjoy.

Although the seed for this book may have been planted more than thirty years ago in my childhood days, three people were mainly responsible for its eventual germination only a few years ago. Joann Iovene continually reminded me of my good intentions to write and draw; Dr. Roger Swain, author, entomologist, and science editor, offered the advice and encouragement that the early manuscript needed; and Cynthia Helms, the children's librarian at the public library in Champaign, Illinois, introduced me to a librarian's view of natural history books.

At the Illinois Natural History Survey, I met a number of entomologists who were happy to "talk insects." Dr. John Bouseman identified some of the beetle larvae that I had collected in rotten logs and supplied me with whirligig beetles as models for drawing; Dr. Dan Fischer suggested watching bagworms to learn about their bag-making techniques; Dr. George Godfrey located the viceroy pupa that posed for one of my illustrations; and Dr. Don Webb identified several of the true flies that are pictured in this book.

Insects are discussed with equal enthusiasm in the Department of Entomology at the University of Illinois. Professor Ellis MacLeod has an insatiable curiosity and a vast knowledge of the natural world. I obtained answers to many of my questions about insects from him, and several models for the illustrations in this book came from his collection. Professor William Horsfall shared his knowledge of mosquitoes with me, and Professor Gil Waldbauer passed on information about the habits of bagworms. Professor Judy Willis told me about her encounters with praying mantises, and in the midst of an Illinois winter, Nathan Schiff supplied me with just the insect I needed from a drawer of his massive insect collection.

The town in which I live, Urbana-Champaign, Illinois, is a community where many people place a high priority on preserving our natural heritage. Lois Drury and Katie Hamrick have long been unflagging supporters of conservation and nature education. For advice on these matters, few people can surpass these two in experience, enthusiasm, and their willingness to share them. I am grateful for their support.

Typing is such a laborious experience for me that I hope Lorie Hatfield, Jim Poepsel, and Kelly Monahan realize how many unpleasant hours with a typewriter they saved me.

I would like to thank the staff at Iowa State University Press for being such helpful partners in this endeavor. Robert Schultz, the Acquisitions Editor, found the home for my manuscript; Bill Silag, the Managing Editor, coordinated the editing; and Lynne Bishop is the editor who so carefully oversaw the refining of my original manuscript.

Finally, I am grateful to all those people who have a reverence for the land and its creatures. As long as this reverence endures, there is hope that we shall continue to share this beautiful planet with its remarkable insects and spiders for many more millenia.

"*To find new things, take the path you took yesterday.*"
—JOHN BURROUGHS

5 mm

I.1.

INTRODUCTION

THIS BOOK is about nature's unsung heroes. In our human infatuation with large animals, we often tend to overlook and underestimate the significance of those small animals with segmented bodies and jointed legs. Just as most of us are unaware of their comings and goings, insects and spiders go about their own affairs, oblivious that humans build supercomputers and travel in supersonic jets.

The abundance alone of insects and their relatives should hint that their obscure lives are nevertheless closely interwoven with our own lives as well as the lives of the other creatures who share this earth. What insects and their relatives lack in size they compensate for in numbers. Mites and springtails of the soil can number over 900 million per acre; the number of descendants of a single female aphid can total 500 billion in a single year. The proliferation of these little animals puts the proverbial rabbit to shame—by their standards, the human population of the world (pushing a mere 5 billion) is miniscule.

Although many habitats on earth are devoid of human life, very few are devoid of all life. Practically every spot on the face of our planet offers a refuge to at least one of the tiny forms of life. Not even hot springs or bleak mountains are without insect or spider life. With far more generations of experience to their credit than ours, these small creatures have found that just about any habitat can be colonized. Fortunately, therefore, we do not need to visit city zoos or distant parks to observe these small, little-known creatures for they can be found in our homes, yards, gardens, or nearby woods.

The earth's small animals are rich in diversity and life styles, and there are an inestimable number of species still to be discovered if we do not thoughtlessly destroy their habitats in the headlong rush to satisfy our craving for wealth and power. Much about these creatures passes unnoticed and unappreciated simply for lack of careful observation. Closer encounters with these species can open new windows and new doors for all of us—with remarkable views of some smaller worlds.

Arthropod Names

CLASSIFICATIONS are based on similarities among creatures. What all the animals in this book have in common is that all of them have jointed legs. This is not the only feature that they share, but it was considered important enough to be used in naming these animals.

Sometimes having only one feature in common is sufficient reason to group a number of creatures together, but almost invariably there are exceptions. Sometimes several characteristics have to be examined before we can be certain of a creature's identity.

Another important consideration in naming creatures is the choice of a language that is acceptable to speakers of all languages. Two ancient languages—Greek and Latin—have been used for centuries as the universal languages. You will find that the formal, scientific names for animals (as opposed to our common names for them) are derived from one or more Greek or Latin words. Whenever one of these formal names is used in this book, it will be followed by its English translation.

After similarities among creatures as well as languages were considered, the name that was finally chosen for these animals with jointed legs was arthropods (*arthron*, joint; *poda*, feet). Arthropods belong to the phylum (*phylon*, tribe) Arthropoda.

Not all arthropods have the same number of legs; they are further divided into classes according to the number of their legs. Those with six legs are insects (class Insecta or class Hexapoda: *hex*, six; *poda*, feet); those with eight legs are spiders, mites, or daddy longlegs (class Arachnida: *arachna*, spider); those that have at least five pairs of legs or other appendages used for walking or swimming are crustaceans (class Crustacea: *crusta*, hard shell). However, millipedes and centipedes (class Myriapoda: *myrios*, very numerous; *poda*, feet) hold the record for numbers of legs—anywhere from 14 to almost 200 pairs.

Perhaps you are getting the hang of this naming scheme. The *phylum* of arthropods is divided into a few *classes;* each class into *orders;* each order into *families;* each family into *genera* (kinds); and, finally, each genus (singular of genera) into *species.*

At the end of each chapter, the names of the class, the order, and the family for each arthropod discussed in the chapter are provided. Those of you who would like more specific information on naming can turn to any number of field guides, several of which are listed under Additional Reading at the back of the book.

Arthropod Numbers

VARIETY AMONG the arthropods is unmatched by any other group of animals or plants. If we draw a circle to represent all the species of animals on our planet, arthropods would take up a whopping chunk of this circle (Fig. I.2). While arthropods represent 80% of the world's animal species, insects represent about 85% of all

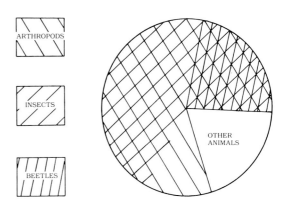

I.2.   THE WORLD OF ARTHROPODS.

arthropods, and beetles represent 35% of the insects. New species of arthropods are constantly being discovered, and each year estimates of the total number of species increase. One entomologist (*entomon,* insect; *logy,* study of) has recently proposed that there may be as many as 12 million species of beetles alone. Insects may not be the biggest creatures on earth, but superlatives certainly suit many of their other features.

Arthropod Skeletons

ARTHROPODS are usually hard and crunchy because their skeletons (also called exoskeletons, cuticles, shells, or skins) are on the outside rather than on the inside like our own.

As arthropods grow, they eventually become too large for their skeletons. They must then shed (or molt) their old skeletons and grow new and larger ones. This molting can occur many times in the life of an arthropod. The immature forms of certain arthropods—spiders, millipedes, centipedes, mites, and many crustaceans—look like miniature adults as they grow and molt. The skeletons of other arthropods—certain insects—also change, but very little, as they grow from immature forms called nymphs to full-grown adults. Still other insects, however, undergo dramatic changes in the forms of their skeletons as they pass from larvae to pupae and finally to adults. We will learn more about these immature insects called nymphs, larvae, and pupae in the pages to come.

Each part of an arthropod's skeleton has its own name. Scientists have names for all the bumps, grooves, and spines on the skeletons of both young and old arthropods; but we will consider just the main parts of their bodies.

We can see these parts in the spider and the fly that have met on the blackberry leaf (Fig. I.3). All insects, such as the fly, have three main body regions: a head at the front, a thorax (*thorax,* breastplate) in the middle, an abdomen (*abdomen,* belly) at the rear. All spiders have two main body regions: a head that is fused with a thorax called a cephalothorax (*cephalus,* head) and an abdomen. In spiders the eight legs are attached to the cephalothorax; in insects the six legs and the wings are always attached to the thorax. Eyes and mouths are found on the first region of

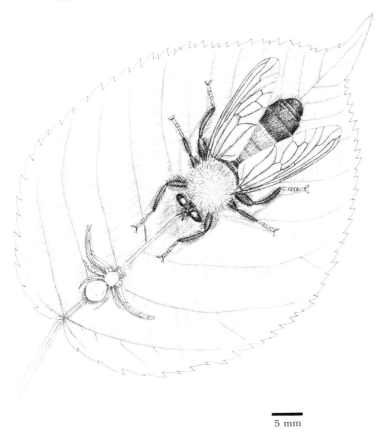

5 mm

the body in both spiders and insects. Insects have mouthparts modified for either sucking or chewing; spiders have jaws tipped with sharp fangs. Insects and other arthropods have antennae but spiders do not. Some of the functions of the antennae are taken over by pedipalps (*pedi*, foot; *palpus*, feeler), which can be found between the first legs and the jaws of spiders.

Arthropod Sizes

WHILE THE SIZES of mammals like ourselves range from 31,000 millimeters (whales) to 50 millimeters (shrews), the sizes of arthropods cover an equally broad spectrum but on a scale that is 200-fold smaller. Not surprisingly, some of the smallest (¼ of a millimeter) and some of the largest (160 millimeters) arthropods are found among that very versatile group—the beetles. Neither of these beetles appears in this book, but the 90-millimeter praying mantis that does appear is among the larger arthropods found on land or in fresh water; another insect in this book—the 1-millimeter book louse—is certainly one of the smaller arthropods. After all, one cannot be very large to live between the pages of a book. The sizes of arthropods seem to be tailored for the worlds in which they live.

All the illustrations of arthropods are accompanied by a scale (bar in millimeters, mm) to give you an idea of just how large or just how small each arthropod is. There is a ruler on the back cover that will help you understand the measurements.

Arthropod Watching

ARTHROPODS are easy to find, easy to watch, and are a source of endless discovery. Although you do not need any special equipment to watch them, you can sometimes get a better view of their worlds by using magnifiers and microscopes (Fig. I.4).

In using a hand lens, hold it about 2 inches from your eye and about the same distance from the creature you are examining. You can focus by moving either the lens or the specimen. A hand lens or a plastic box with a magnifying lid can be

I.4. MAGNIFIERS.

A. HAND LENS

B. MAGNIFYING PLASTIC BOX

C. STEREOMICROSCOPE

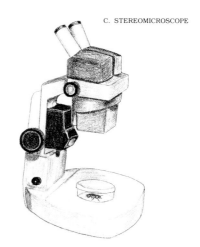

brought on all field trips and used for closer looks as you walk along. With one of these, you can magnify the image of an arthropod 3–10 times its actual size.

A stereomicroscope is an instrument that gives you a three-dimensional view of small creatures and enlarges each image 10–50 times. Place a small creature in a clear plastic or glass container while you watch it, and then return it to its habitat after you have enjoyed observing it at close range. You can use these at schools and nature centers, or you can purchase them from a local store or from one of the supply houses, listed in the Appendix in the back of the book, to use at home.

With this introduction to spiders, insects, and their relatives, you have the basic information to begin exploring a world very different from our own in many ways. And a good place to start is right at home.

CLASSIFICATION

Class Arachnida
    Spiders
        Order Araneida (*aranea*, spider)
            Family Thomisidae (*thomis*, thread): **crab spider**

Class Insecta
    Beetles
        Order Coleoptera (*coleos*, sheath; *ptera*, wings)
            Family Lucanidae (*lucanus*, a kind of beetle): **stag beetle**
    True Flies
        Order Diptera (*dis*, two; *ptera*, wings)
            Family Asilidae (*asilus*, gadfly): **robber fly**

Close Encounters with Insects and Spiders

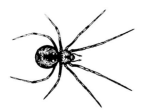

1.1.

1. *Home, School, and Garden*

OUR HOMES AND SCHOOLS are not strictly ours alone. In stacks of old newspapers, cabinets, corners, and sinks, we probably have overlooked tenants that never pay rent. Even our pets have boarders. These are creatures that have forsaken their native homes; they are immigrants from the forests and fields that have sought refuge in our homes and schools. They have thrived and multiplied in our company. And, if we in turn fail to appreciate some of their ways, we still cannot claim that they are unworthy of our curiosity.

Tucked away in corners of the house are the humble webs of **cobweb spiders** (Fig. 1.2). Sometimes a little less cleaning in these corners

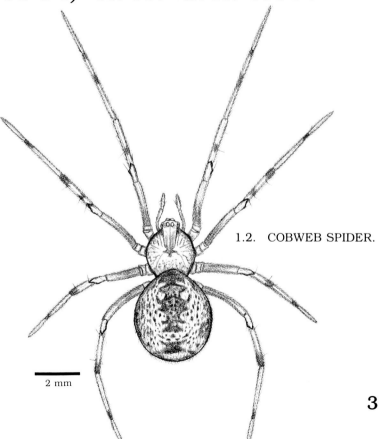

1.2. COBWEB SPIDER.

2 mm

3

pays off—especially when it means sparing the spiders and their webs. Cobwebs may lack the elegant weave of other webs, but they can still snare a good number of flies, moths, and mosquitoes.

Even though each cobweb spider has eight eyes, it perceives the world better with its sense of touch than with its vision. Its long legs are very sensitive to vibrations, and an amorous male will court a female by plucking the threads of her web. Of course, he must be careful to inform her that he has arrived as a suitor—and not as a morsel of food.

If you place a cobweb spider in your terrarium or a clear plastic box, within a few hours or a day, the spider will spin its web—not a fancy or ornate web but one that nevertheless suits the spider's purposes very well (Fig. 1.3). Now you can add one or more flies or small moths. Eventually a moth or fly will bump into the web and the spider will dash forth to secure its catch. Watch how the spider manipulates its prey. It will spin out silk from its spinnerets and then comb this silk over its captive with bristles at the end of its last pair of legs.

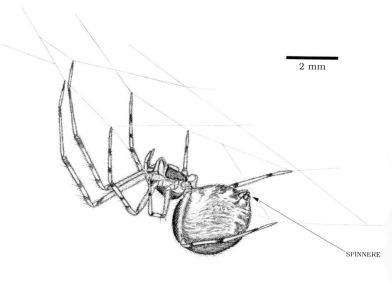

2 mm

SPINNERE

1.3. COBWEB SPIDER ON HER WEB.

Some morning you may share your bathroom with a fuzzy little fly that will restlessly strut and spin on the edge of the sink. Decked out in all its fuzz, the **moth fly** looks more like a tiny moth than the fly that it really is (Fig. 1.4). Do not be startled by its sudden appearance. It has spent the last few weeks as an egg, larva, and pupa in the depths of the drain pipe.

1.4. MOTH FLY.

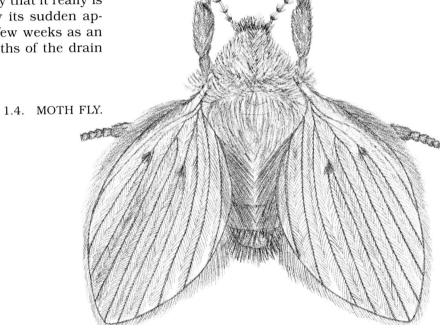

1 mm

Everyone has encountered **fleas** at one time or another, but few people know the flea other than as an elusive brown speck that scurries through the hair of their pet. This particular flea, in fact, was found on the nose of my cat who posed for the drawing at the beginning of this chapter. Upon examining the flea at close range, you can see how well-suited it is for its environment (Fig. 1.5).

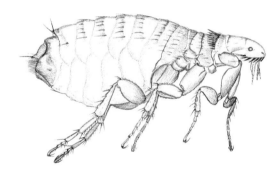

1 mm

Broad vertically, but slim horizontally, the flea has a physique that allows it to wind its way through dense fur. Its antennae lie in grooves behind the eyes where they cannot snag on hairs; hooked claws help it maintain its grip as it navigates in a sea of hair.

Fleas have probably shared our quarters since humans first took up housekeeping. Fleas cannot tolerate a nomadic life and need the security of a home—be it only a nest, a burrow, or a cave—where their larvae can feed on dust and debris until they are ready to mature and begin dining on the richer fare of blood.

You can do a favor for your dog or cat by catching one of its fleas, or at least trying to catch one of its fleas. The flea easily sidles among the hairs and avoids the grip of your fingers. Its many bristles and recurved claws anchor it firmly to the tangle of hairs. As you will soon discover, a flea is difficult to catch.

1.5. CAT FLEA.

Silverfish are some of the few insects, other than moths and butterflies, that are covered with scales (Fig. 1.6). These insect scales, like those on fish, are arranged on the surface of the silverfish just as shingles are arranged on a roof. The color pattern of each animal arises from a mosaic of tiny scales of different colors and shapes.

Silverfish also go by another descriptive name, bristletail. At the head (anterior) end are two very long antennae and at the tail (posterior) end are three equally long and bristly structures known as cerci (*cercus,* tail). Both the antennae and the cerci inform the bristletail about the smell, flavor, and feel of its environment as it crawls among old newspapers indoors or rotting logs outdoors.

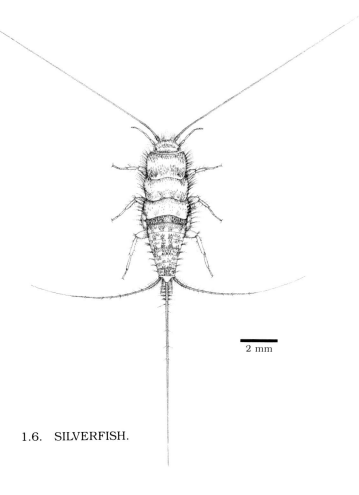

2 mm

1.6.   SILVERFISH.

7

The origins of the **Mediterranean meal moth** are obscure (Fig. 1.7). Its name implies that its ancestors originally came from Europe to the New World; however, it was first noticed in 1879 at a flour mill in Germany that received a good share of its wheat from America. If, indeed, the meal moth originally came from the New World, it probably survived on wild seeds and grains before it discovered our stores of grain.

Dried grain is a spartan environment; cornmeal and flour are as dry as desert sand. In this habitat, however, the caterpillars of the meal moth spin their silken chambers without ever encountering any water other than that which they naturally produce from the breakdown of nutrients in their food.

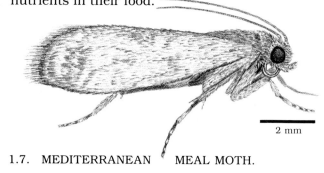

2 mm

1.7. MEDITERRANEAN MEAL MOTH.

1.8. DRUGSTORE BEETLE.

1 mm

Drugstore beetles are as at home in the kitchen pantry as they are in a medicine cabinet. They can show up just about anywhere. They find drug plants to their liking, and they also relish dry groceries, seeds, and leather. I not only

8

found a few beetles in my flour supply but also discovered that one beetle had excavated a tunnel through one of my leather-bound books.

Whenever the privacy of its pantry or medicine cabinet is invaded, the drugstore beetle can play dead by tucking its legs and antennae into matching grooves on its under side (Fig. 1.8). Gently flip a beetle over on its back and poke it with the tip of your pencil. With its legs tucked away, the beetle looks more like a brown sesame seed than a pantry raider.

Although the **cockroach** may not be a particularly popular household insect, it does claim an ancient and impressive lineage (Fig. 1.9). Back in the days when coal swamps covered a good portion of America, 6 inches was a standard size for cockroaches. In the almost 300 million years that have passed, the descendants of the swamp roaches have never matched their ancestors in size. However, they have discovered other habitats to their liking besides swamps. We are best acquainted with the cockroaches that we have as roommates; but there are numerous woodland

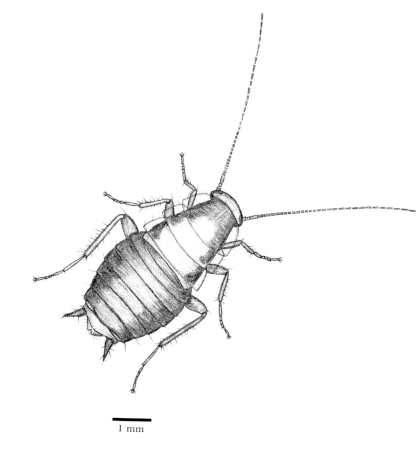

1 mm

1.9. COCKROACH NYMPH.

9

roaches that are as at home under logs and stones as our household roaches are under the kitchen sink.

There is a good reason that a cockroach is so hard to swat or step on. Each of the two cerci at its posterior end is covered with nine rows of hairs that are sensitive to puffs of air from your foot or from your hand, or whatever weapon you choose. Each row of hairs is especially sensitive to air coming from a particular direction and that direction differs from hair row to hair row. So, not only can the cockroach detect a gust of air from a threatening foot, but the hairs of the cerci also tell it where the source of the air (the threat) is located.

Sensations are picked up and processed by the nervous system. Figure 1.10 is a simplified diagram of the chain of clusters of nerve cells that comprise the cockroach nervous system (shaded area). The clusters of nerve cells in the thorax and abdomen are called ganglia; the large cluster in the head is the brain. The cells of our own nervous system are also concentrated in groups, within our very complex brains and spinal cord ganglia.

Information from the hairs on the cerci, re-

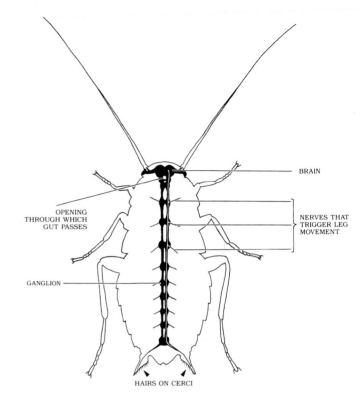

BRAIN

OPENING THROUGH WHICH GUT PASSES

NERVES THAT TRIGGER LEG MOVEMENT

GANGLION

HAIRS ON CERCI

1.10. SIMPLIFIED DIAGRAM OF COCKROACH NERVOUS SYSTEM (*shaded*) AND PATHWAY OF SIGNAL FROM THE RIGHT CERCUS (*white line*).

layed almost instantly from nerve cell to nerve cell until it reaches the brain and the nerves that control the running muscles of the legs, tells the cockroach in which direction it should run. Somehow, all the nerve cells along this pathway (Fig. 1.10, white line) are involved in "making the decision" that the cockroach should run away from the source of the wind.

If the hairs on the cerci are covered or removed, the cockroach ignores the air currents and makes no attempt to escape. Thus, cerci are obviously an important safety feature of cockroach life.

Walking on ceilings is an everyday accomplishment for cockroaches and **flies** (Fig. 1.11). The only human beings that have matched this feat are astronauts who have escaped the gravity of earth. It is the force of gravity that holds us to the earth, and it is this same force that promptly returns us to the floor if we try to walk on ceilings. Since weight is a measure of the force of gravity, the force holding us to the surface of the earth is far greater than the force holding a little

fly, or even a large cockroach. But despite their small sizes, gravity still acts on insects. When they walk on ceilings, this force is counteracted by the slightly greater force of adhesion between the ceiling and the sticky pads on the soles of their feet. Watch a fly walking on the inside of a clear jar, and you will see these white, sticky pads that keep it from falling.

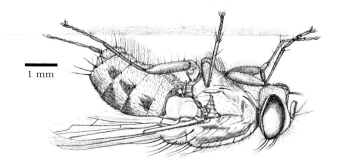

1 mm

1.11. FLESH FLY.

11

In the summer you can often find **hornworm** caterpillars feeding on tomato plants in your garden (Fig. 1.12). Like other caterpillars that will eventually become moths or butterflies, the hornworm can be reared easily. Place one in a large jar or terrarium with a constant supply of fresh leaves from the plant on which you found it feeding. You can even raise a number of caterpillars during the winter by ordering them, along with specially prepared caterpillar food, from one of the biological supply companies listed in the Appendix.

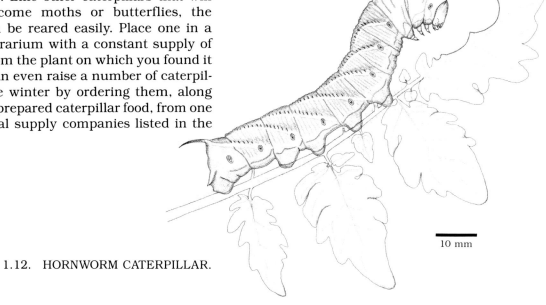

10 mm

1.12.   HORNWORM CATERPILLAR.

All insects and spiders molt as they grow and age. When they outgrow their hard skins, which also happen to be their skeletons, they molt and lay down slightly larger skeletons.

In spiders and insect nymphs, the new skeleton looks very much like the old skeleton, except that a few new structures may appear or a few old structures may disappear. In caterpillars and other larvae, skeletons may not change much for several molts, until suddenly the larva may take on a very different look. This complete metamorphosis (*meta,* change; *morphe,* form; *-sis,* process of) from a larva, to a pupa, and then to an adult is an amazing process; and the more we learn about metamorphosis, the more amazing the whole process seems.

At the time of each molt, old structures break down and the materials are recycled in the formation of new structures; very little is wasted. A new skeleton begins to form just before the old one is shed, so that when the old skin is shed, the new skeleton is still very thin, fragile, and colorless. A newly molted insect is soft and white and especially vulnerable to its enemies. Within a few hours, however, the new skin thickens and darkens, and the insect soon is fully armored to face the rigors of its world.

A hornworm caterpillar grows at a very rapid rate. Only 2–3 weeks pass between the time the egg hatches and the time the caterpillar stops growing. In between, the caterpillar sheds its skin four times (Fig. 1.13). At each molt, it leaves its old skeleton behind and grows until the new skeleton is ready to be shed.

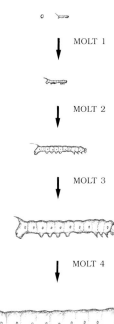

MOLT 1

MOLT 2

MOLT 3

MOLT 4

1.13.   GROWTH OF A HORNWORM.

13

From the time that each caterpillar hatches from its egg, there are groups of cells within it that are destined to form all the structures of the future adult—wings, eyes, legs, antennae, etc. These clusters of presumptive adult structures are called imaginal discs (*imago*, adult). In a sense then, the adult is prepackaged within the larva. When the caterpillar molts to the pupa at metamorphosis, the imaginal discs move from the inside surface of the caterpillar's skin to the outside of the pupa. If you look closely at an area of a full-grown caterpillar (see arrowhead after molt 4 in Fig. 1.13), you will see a white patch beneath the skin. This tissue on both sides of the caterpillar will give rise to the wings of the moth. In the pupa, the same tissue lies on the surface (Fig. 1.14).

Growth of animals and plants is controlled by naturally occurring chemicals called hormones (*hormao*, arouse). In the case of insects, these chemicals are produced in the brain, as well as in other tissues and then distributed by the blood. Periodic growth and molting are coupled to the periodic rise and fall of these hormonal levels.

The hormone levels "tell" the caterpillar when it should stop eating and prepare for its molt to a pupa. Many changes occur within the caterpillar at this time. Not only does it lose its voracious appetite for tomato leaves, but it also crawls down from the plant and begins to wander.

Along the back of the wandering caterpillar, you will now see a long, throbbing green stripe; this is the heart (Fig. 1.15). The blood is green and flows from the posterior end to the anterior end through the long, muscular heart that expands and contracts. Unlike the heart in a large animal that pumps blood into blood vessels, the long, dorsal heart in spiders and insects pumps blood into the spaces that surround other tissues. When the blood reaches the insect's or spider's head, it leaves the heart and flows freely

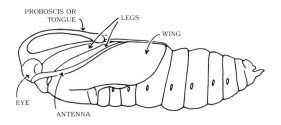

1.14. HORNWORM PUPA.

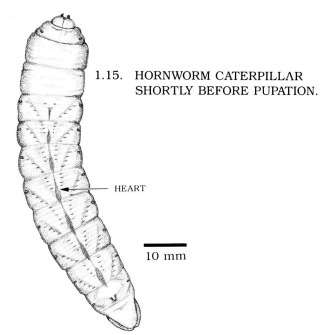

1.15. HORNWORM CATERPILLAR SHORTLY BEFORE PUPATION.

HEART

10 mm

inchcs of soil or sawdust. During its resting period, the tissues within the caterpillar undergo remarkable changes that will eventually transform it into a pupa. About 5 days after the caterpillar burrows underground, it will suddenly shed its old larval skin and unveil its new pupal self (Fig. 1.16).

through the body spaces until it finds its way back to the posterior end of the heart. The blood percolates through these spaces without ever passing through veins, arteries, or capillaries.

The caterpillar roams until it finds a place where it can burrow into the ground and lie undisturbed for several days. If you are rearing a caterpillar, to provide for this need, be sure that the container in which you keep it has at least 2

1.16. HORNWORM PUPA.

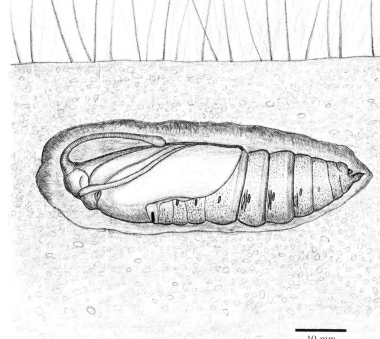

10 mm

Adult moths and butterflies form within the shells of their pupae or, for some, in cocoons containing pupae; some will emerge in a few days or a few weeks, while others will not emerge unless they experience several months of cold winter weather. But they are worth waiting for. If a moth or butterfly does not appear from a pupa after 6 weeks at room temperature, leave it outside or on a cold window ledge until spring. By then it should be ready to emerge.

In anticipation of the appearance of the moth or butterfly, be certain that it has a vertical object, such as a stick or even a towel that it can climb as soon as it sheds the pupal skin (Fig. 1.17). From the vertical perch it can then pump blood into its small, wrinkled wings and prepare for its first flight.

1.17.   NEWLY EMERGED SPHINX MOTHS.

16

A **sphinx moth** (Figs. 1.17, 1.18) will emerge from the pupal shell of the hornworm. You might mix a tablespoon of sugar in a glass of water and wet your finger with the sugar water and offer some to the moth before you give it its freedom. This moth, like most moths and butterflies, will then fly off to sip nectar from flowers and will eventually mate. Some moths, however, such as the large silk moths, have their last meals as caterpillars and fly off only to mate and lay eggs.

If the moth you have reared happens to be a female and if her cage is outdoors or near an open window with a screen, you might witness a remarkable sight after the sun sets on the day of her emergence. Female moths produce a perfume known as pheromone (*phero*, carry; *moneo*, inform) that can attract males of the same species from miles around. Sometime during the night, you might find several of these males flapping against the cage. Moths and other insects have their keen sense of smell located on their antennae; for them, "Beauty is in the antennae of the beholder," as one scientist recently put it.

10 mm

1.18.   SPHINX MOTH.

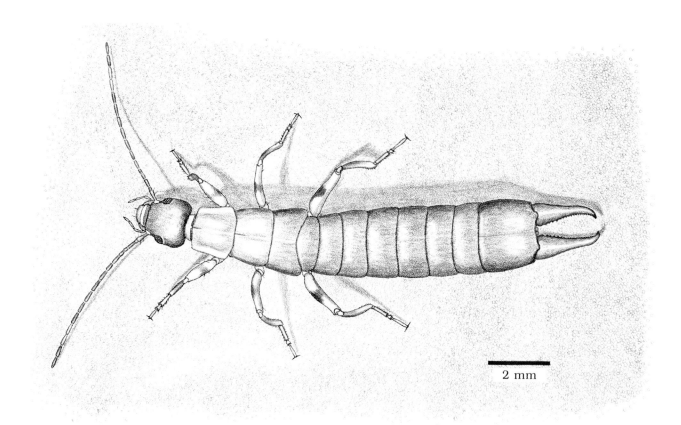

1.19. FEMALE EARWIG.

2 mm

18

European earwigs traveled across the Atlantic to the New World with some of the early settlers. Although the old superstition that earwigs make themselves at home in people's ears also traveled across the Atlantic with these insects, you will not find earwigs in such places. Instead, they make themselves at home in yards, gardens, and buildings.

You can tell the earwig in Figure 1.19 is a female by the relatively straight shape of her pincers. The pincers of a male look very different—they are more curved (Fig. 1.20).

Once the earwigs mature and mate at the end of summer, the male's mission is completed, but the female's is only beginning. Before winter arrives, she will retire to a little cavern that she digs in the soil. Here she will lay anywhere from 10 to 60 eggs and will remain with them until they hatch in the spring. Her maternal concerns do not end until the young reach their first molt. Until then she guards her brood and feeds them whatever vegetable matter she can scavenge nearby.

Earwigs seem just as at home in a terrarium with a layer of damp soil and a little plant litter as they do in a garden. Pieces of vegetables and some dog food can be added for food, but remove them when they start to mold. Earwigs will go about their everyday affairs in the terrarium, and females will probably find many suitable places under leaves or stones for their nurseries. By gently lifting some of these leaves and stones, you may catch a glimpse of a mother and her brood.

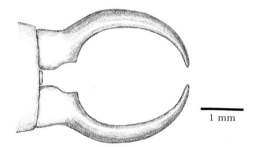

1 mm

1.20.   CURVED PINCERS OF MALE EARWIG.

Mud daubers are gentle, artistic wasps with a flair for sculpting mud. The **pipe-organ mud dauber** (Fig. 1.21) is blue-black with white-stockinged hind legs. Although these mud daubers sometimes build their nests as their ancestors did, on cliffs or in hollow trees, they seem to prefer building their pipe organs on the sides of our porches, bridges, and barns.

Once a dauber sets about building, it diligently persists for hours. Load after load of mud balls is flown from puddles, ponds, and streams, and each load is molded into one of the many parallel strips that make up each pipe. After some 30 or 40 loads of mud, the female dauber begins a new routine. She has just completed the construction of a length of pipe that will be the nursery for one of her children. She will place in this chamber of the pipe several spiders that she paralyzes with her sting (Fig. 1.22). These living,

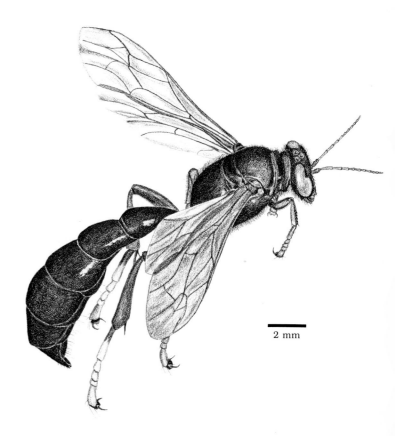

2 mm

1.21.   PIPE-ORGAN MUD DAUBER.

20

but paralyzed, spiders will be the provisions for a dauber larva. After a single egg is laid in the chamber, the female returns to her mud-daubing routine until a new chamber is ready for more spiders. And so it goes until mud, spiders, or eggs are gone. In the pipe-organ nest shown here, the wasp larva in the right pipe has already eaten its spiders, pupated, and chewed its way through the mud wall. This nest has a total of 11 chambers, and a view inside one of the chambers shows paralyzed spiders that have not yet been eaten by the dauber larva.

If you would like to provide an additional source of building material for the female dauber, you can add a small amount of water and food coloring to a bare patch of soil in the yard. If colored strips start to appear in her nest and if you find her foot prints and jaw prints in your mud patch, then you know that she has found it.

You might also add a little honey for the dauber. Refreshments are always appreciated.

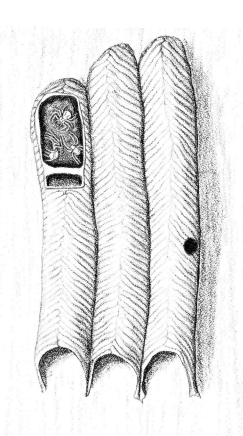

1.22.   PIPES OF MUD DAUBER WITH
PARALYZED SPIDERS IN A CHAMBER.

10 mm

CLASSIFICATION

Class Arachnida
    Spiders
        Order Araneida (*aranea*, spider)
            Family Theridiidae (*theridion*, beast): **cobweb spider**

Class Insecta
    Silverfish (Bristletails)
        Order Thysanura (*thysanos*, fringe; *oura*, tail)
            Family Lepismatidae (*lepisma*, scale): **silverfish**

    Grasshoppers, Crickets, Cockroaches, Mantises, Walkingsticks
        Order Orthoptera (*orthos*, straight; *ptera*, wings)
            Family Blattidae (*blatta*, cockroach): **cockroach**

    Earwigs
        Order Dermaptera (*derma*, skin; *ptera*, wings)
            Family Forficulidae (*forficula*, little scissors): **European earwig**

    Fleas
        Order Siphonaptera (*siphon*, tube; *aptera*, wingless)
            Family Pulicidae (*pulex*, flea): **cat flea**

    True Flies
        Order Diptera (*dis*, two; *ptera*, wings)
            Family Psychodidae (*psyche*, moth, butterfly;-*odes*, like): **moth fly**
            Family Sarcophagidae (*sarcos*, flesh; *phagos*, eater): **flesh fly**

Beetles
    Order Coleoptera (*coleos*, sheath; *ptera*, wings)
        Family Anobiidae (*ano*, over; *bios*, life): **drugstore beetle**

Butterflies, Moths
    Order Lepidoptera (*lepidos*, scale; *ptera*, wings)
        Family Pyralidae (*pyralis*, an insect that is said to live in fire): **Mediterranean meal moth**
        Family Sphingidae (*Sphinx*, a mythological monster who asked riddles and who held its head like the hornworm on p. 12): **sphinx moth** and **hornworm**

Ants, Bees, Wasps
    Order Hymenoptera (*hymen*, membrane; *ptera*, wings)
        Family Sphecidae (*sphex*, wasp): **pipe-organ mud dauber**

2.1.

2. Ponds and Streams

AT ALL TIMES of the year you can find small creatures in ponds and streams. The types and ages of creatures may vary with the seasons, but some will always be moving about, even on the hottest days of summer or the bleakest days of winter. Regardless of how cold the air temperature is, and even if ice has formed, the temperature under the ice will never drop below freezing.

Visit a pond or stream with a kitchen strainer, a jar, and a tray or pan. Sweeping the strainer through pondweeds, over submerged rocks, or through the mud and sand will bring up a good selection of wriggling creatures, unless the water is exceptionally polluted. For a closer look at these creatures, gently place some of them in your pan of water. They will stand out particularly well in a white pan. Return the rest of the creatures in the strainer to the water.

Some of the animals that you find are so unusual and so unlike the creatures that we encounter on land that you might want to spend more time watching them in an aquarium (Fig. 2.2).

A standard pet store aquarium or a large, widemouthed jar will serve equally well as an aquarium for little creatures from ponds and streams. Place a layer of soil about 1 inch deep on the bottom of your container, overlay this with another inch of sand or gravel, uproot a few water plants from the shallow water and push the roots into the soil layer, and add several inches of water from the stream or pond. This

2.2. COLLECTING AND OBSERVING AQUATIC INSECTS.

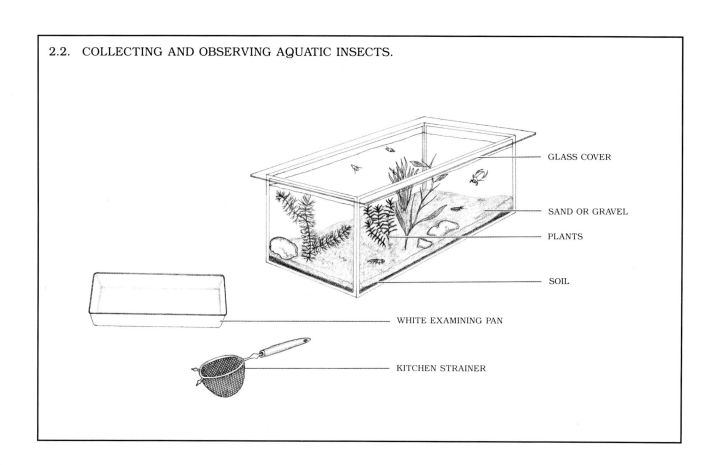

GLASS COVER

SAND OR GRAVEL

PLANTS

SOIL

WHITE EXAMINING PAN

KITCHEN STRAINER

water will contain many of the microscopic plants and animals that some of the aquatic insects eat. You can then fill the aquarium to the top with water from a faucet and then cover to prevent evaporation.

The aquatic plants remove carbon dioxide and provide oxygen; microscopic life provides food for smaller herbivores and carnivores; and in turn, smaller insects and invertebrates provide food for the larger insect predators. After placing a sheet of glass over the top of the aquarium, you should have a balanced, self-contained minipond or ministream.

Living in a pond or stream presents a challenge to insects and their relatives that is not encountered on land—how to obtain the oxygen that is just as essential for life in water as it is for life on land. First, consider how land-dwelling insects breathe and then see how their method has been modified for life underwater.

On land, insects and spiders breathe through special pores called spiracles (*spiraculum*, air hole) located along their sides. From the spira-

cles, hollow, silvery tubes called tracheae (*tracheia*, windpipe) carry air to the internal organs. These air tubes are actually inpocketings of the animal's water-repellent exoskeleton, and their linings are shed whenever the spider or insect molts. Look inside an empty cicada shell (p. 153) and you will see a number of these twisted tubes. These tracheal tubes repeatedly branch inside the insect to form treelike networks of progressively smaller air tubes until even the most remote cells of the animal are supplied with oxygen.

The spiracles on the surface of the tobacco hornworm are quite conspicuous (Fig. 2.3, black dots); if we could trace the tracheae that begin at the spiracles, we would see a ladderlike pattern similar to the one in Figure 2.3. The finest branches of the air tubes, however, are so small and so numerous they cannot be shown in the diagram.

2.3 SPIRACLES AND TRACHEAE OF A HORNWORM.

The respiratory systems of other insects and spiders are variations of this basic caterpillar plan, and many of these variations can be found in the insects that live in ponds and streams.

As we discuss the various creatures we are likely to find on a visit to a pond or stream, we will point out how each of them manages to get the oxygen that it needs.

Divers and Swimmers

SCIENTISTS TELL US that the ancestors of all life on earth came from the sea, first colonizing the land and then the inland streams, lakes, and ponds. The Cherokee Indians, however, have a somewhat different version of the earth's history.

They claim that from nothingness, the Great Spirit created a vast sea and sky, and into this world He brought many animals that were at home in the sea or in the sky. But without Grandmother Earth, the Great Spirit and all the animals that swam in the sea or flew in the sky were dissatisfied. From all the water animals, the Great Spirit chose the diving beetle to dive to the bottom of the great sea in search of land. With the little ball of mud that the diving beetle brought back, the Great Spirit molded the land masses of Grandmother Earth.

2.4.   DIVING BEETLE.

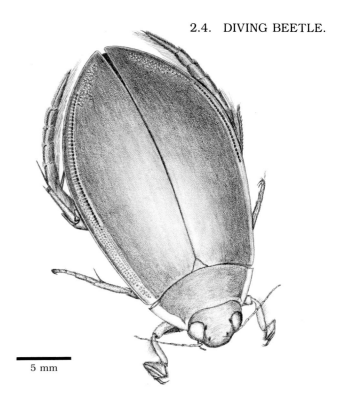

5 mm

The tale of the **diving beetle** reflects the esteem in which the Cherokee Indians held this little creature of their ponds and lakes. Perhaps they reasoned that the Great Spirit would only choose a very special creature, beautifully suited for life in the water. The diving beetle is certainly that (Fig. 2.4).

With hind legs shaped like oar blades and with sleek, streamlined bodies, diving beetles are unsurpassed among aquatic beetles for their grace and speed. Although diving beetle larvae do not master the art of diving until they reach adulthood, they master underwater hunting at an early age. Adults and larvae alike have healthy appetites for any insect, snail, fish, or tadpole that they are fast enough and strong enough to subdue.

The diving beetle is also as well prepared for courtship as it is for hunting. Throughout his nuptial swim, the male must maintain a firm hold on his swift and wet partner. The sleek body of the female presents a definite problem for the male, but with suction cups on his two front feet, he eventually "comes to grips" with his slippery mate. With a little magnification, you can see the round suction cups on the soles of his broad feet.

Adult diving beetles have spiracles that open between their abdomens and their wing cases (Fig. 2.5). Each time a beetle surfaces, it sticks the end of its abdomen out of the water and collects air beneath its wing case for its next dive.

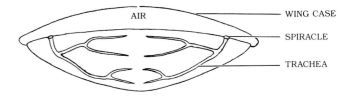

2.5. CROSS SECTION OF THE ABDOMEN OF A DIVING BEETLE.

The dragonlike larvae of diving beetles also pierce the surface of the water with the tips of their abdomens to replenish their air supplies, but these larvae snorkel through only one pair of spiracles rather than breathing through many pairs like the adult beetles. **Diving beetle larvae** (Fig. 2.6) are just one of a number of water-dwelling insects with long tails and snorkels. Many fly larvae that lie on the bottom of the pond in shallow stretches near shore have telescoping snorkels that stretch and shrink depending on the depth of the water.

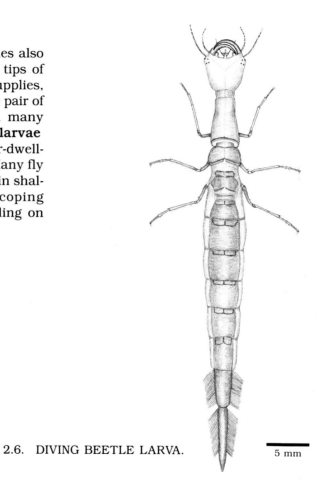

2.6. DIVING BEETLE LARVA.

5 mm

When it comes to diving, the **crawling water beetle** is no match for the diving beetle. Its wobbly efforts are almost comical by comparison, and the contrast between the gracefulness of the two beetles reminds one of the contrast between the ungainly gait of a newborn colt and the graceful gallop of its mother.

A crawling water beetle traps the air supply for its dives under two plates on its belly. Actually, each plate is the unusually wide, flat, first segment of this beetle's hind leg. In Figure 2.7 you can see the right hind leg of the beetle between the belly plate and the wing cover.

2.7. CRAWLING WATER BEETLE.

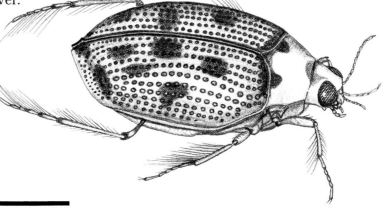

1 mm

31

There are two true bugs of the pond that use their two hind legs as oars. One swims on its back and is appropriately named the **backswimmer**; the other bug swims on its belly and is called a water boatman. Notice how these bugs and boats share the same shape.

The backswimmer (Fig. 2.8) carries its air supply on its belly. When a backswimmer floats to the surface, the long hairs folded over its belly suddenly unfurl and float on the surface of the water (Fig. 2.9). Each long, thin hair has a wettable half and a waxy, nonwettable half. The wettable surfaces of the hairs cling to the surface of the water, but the waxy surfaces of the hairs only contact the air. When the backswimmer pushes off from the surface of the pond, it cannot dive without the long hairs folding back over its belly and trapping a glistening pocket of air next to the waxy surface of its belly hairs.

As the water boatman rows through the water, its entire body glistens from the blanket of air

2.8. BACKSWIMMER.

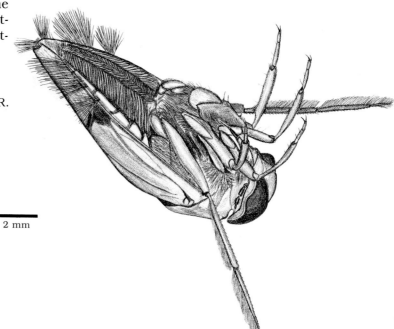

2 mm

32

that wraps around it. Thousands of tiny hairs, wettable only at their tips, coat the surface of the boatman's body and hold the blanket of air in place.

Drop a fly in front of a backswimmer or offer it a tiny piece of hamburger on the end of a stick. It will quickly become accustomed to accepting snacks from you.

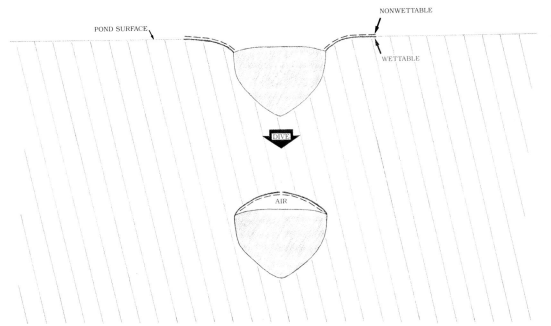

2.9. DIAGRAMMATIC CROSS SECTIONS OF BACKSWIMMER TRAPPING AIR FOR A DIVE.

Before the last traces of ice have vanished, **fairy shrimp** make their debut in the pond (Fig. 2.10). They are crustaceans like the shrimp of the oceans and the wood lice of the land but have adapted to icy waters that few of the other pond creatures find appealing. At this time of year, frogs and fish are still too cold and drowsy to consider making a meal of fairy shrimp, so these tiny, pastel crustaceans glide through the water undisturbed.

One cannot help but marvel at the workings of the tiny nervous system that is responsible for the movements of this most graceful of pond crustaceans. The two rows of feathery gills on the belly of the fairy shrimp do not beat in unison but rather move in ripples from head to tail. By peering into the pond, you can easily observe these movements, since fairy shrimp always swim on their backs, their gills pointing skyward. Only the rippling gaits of centipedes and millipedes can rival the style and complexity of gill locomotion in the fairy shrimp.

To be small is not necessarily to be simple. The fairy shrimp simply makes ample use of what it has. Its gills are used not only for breathing and swimming, but they also set up

34

2.10.   MALE FAIRY SHRIMP.

1 mm

currents that channel food particles to its mouth. The antennae sample the odors of the pond, and they also take on a special role in the love affairs of the fairy shrimp. In the male those formidable, facial tusks are actually antennae that have been adapted for embracing the larger female during courtship and mating.

By early or mid-April, the fairy shrimp find the rising temperature of the pond water too warm. With their courtship finished and their eggs deposited, they disappear from the pond as quickly as they appeared. Only their eggs remain on the bottom of the pond, awaiting the coming of next spring.

Crawlers

SCOOP SOME MUD from the shallow end of a pond or overturn a rock in a stream if you are in search of the creatures who do more crawling than diving and swimming.

In flowing waters you will find that the creatures clinging to the stones do not offer much resistance to the current. They are flat and low-lying; even mountain torrents cannot loosen their firm grips from the stones.

On its top (dorsal) surface, the copper-colored **water penny** (Fig. 2.11) reminds one of another creature called a chiton that lives on the wave-beaten shores of oceans. The water penny, however, is the larva of a beetle, and the chiton is a relative of clams and snails.

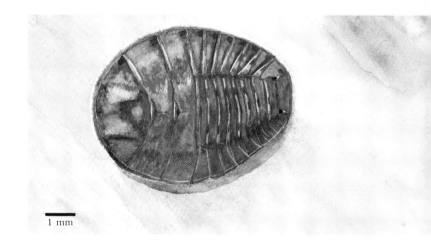

1 mm

2.11. DORSAL SURFACE OF A WATER PENNY.

One look at its lower (ventral) surface will reveal the various hallmarks of an insect (Fig. 2.12).

There are many aquatic larvae, pupae, and nymphs that breathe without any spiracles like those found on other insects and spiders. Instead, they have gills like fairy shrimp (p. 34) that are filled with fine air tubes. Whenever the oxygen level in the gills drops below the oxygen level in the surrounding water, the imbalance is automatically corrected by a process known as diffusion. During diffusion, oxygen dissolved in the water passes through the surface membrane of each gill and into the air tubes. Look for leaflike gills on the nymphs of mayflies and damselflies; on stonefly nymphs, water pennies, and dobson fly larvae, you will see hairlike gills.

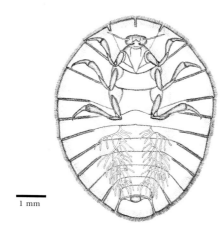

1 mm

2.12.   VENTRAL SURFACE OF A WATER PENNY.

The water penny is one aquatic insect that never surfaces for air until its larval and pupal days are over. How does it get the oxygen it needs?

2.13. DOBSON FLY LARVA.

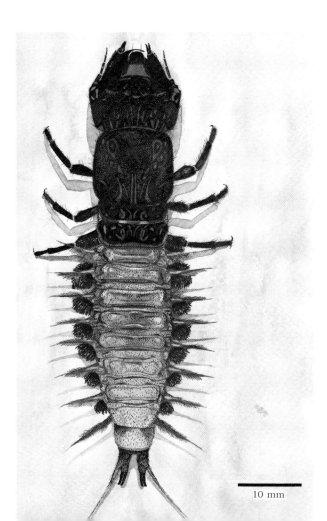

10 mm

The **dobson fly larva** (Fig. 2.13) is an exception to the rule for the presence of gills; it has spiracles as well as gills and can survive ashore for many hours if necessary.

To reach its impressive size of about 80 mm, the larva of the dobson fly spends 3 years in a stream before coming ashore as an insect with large, lacy wings. Dobson fly larvae are best observed and left in their home streams; if placed in an aquarium, they will promptly devour all the other creatures in sight. If you find one under a stone in the stream, it will dig in with the grappling hooks at the posterior end of its abdomen and quickly scuttle backward. And watch out for those jaws!

As adults, caddis flies look like small, drab moths with long antennae; in their youth, they look like caterpillars. But very few true caterpillars live in streams or ponds and build their own portable homes as do **caddis worms.** With grains of sand, pieces of leaves, thin sticks, or tiny snail shells, caddis worms build cases (Fig. 2.14) in which they spend all their days as larvae and pupae.

During its travels, a caddis worm waves its abdomen to circulate water over hairlike gills while, like the larva of the tiger beetle (p. 157), maintaining a good grip on its home with the pair of sturdy hooks on its abdomen. As they grow and molt, they simply remodel and expand their cases by adding material to the entrances. Instinct determines their choices of building materials and architectural styles. In fact, caddis worms are easier to identify from the forms of their cases than from the forms of their bodies.

If you have some caddis worms in your aquarium, try adding various building materials that they might use: sand grains of different colors, pieces of different leaves, tiny twigs, or grass stems. See how picky caddis worms are about the colors and textures of materials they use to remodel their cases.

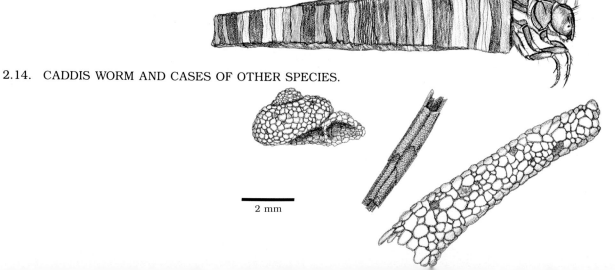

2.14. CADDIS WORM AND CASES OF OTHER SPECIES.

2 mm

Nymphs of three insect orders—the stoneflies (Fig. 2.15), the mayflies, as well as the damselflies and dragonflies—pass the winter months beneath the ice in streams and ponds. They may spend several months or as many as several years in the water; three years is the record for mayflies and stoneflies, and some dragonfly nymphs may spend 5 years on the bottom of a pond. However, their days are numbered once they leave the water, for their travels on land are ephemeral by comparison. Dragonflies and damselflies may fly over the pond for several weeks, but adult mayflies and many adult stoneflies never eat a single meal; they die as soon as they finish mating and egg laying.

Because their lives on land are so very different from their lives in the water, the nymphs of these insects often do not look very much like

2.15. STONEFLY NYMPH.

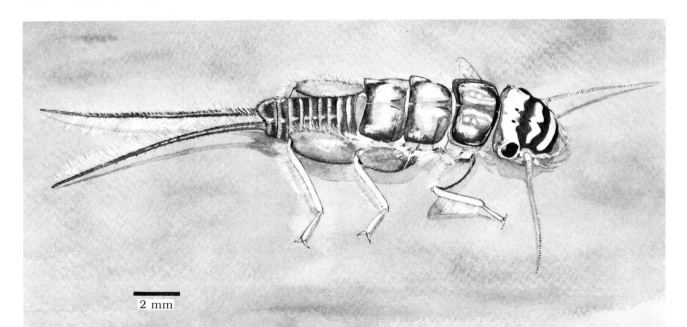

2 mm

39

the adults. In this respect, they are not like the nymphs of land insects that look like miniature versions of the adults. Entomologists often refer to them as naiads (*Naias,* a water nymph) to distinguish them from other insect nymphs. Since naiads, like larvae, undergo obvious changes in form before becoming adults, we might ask what makes these aquatic nymphs different from larvae?

Before becoming adults, larvae must first become pupae. At this time, the future wings of the adult insect move from the inside of the larva to the outside of the pupa. Nymphs do not go through a pupal stage. The future wings of the adult form and grow on the outside of the nymph. Note the small, fledgling wings on naiads and other nymphs and their absence from the surface of larvae.

On damselfly and mayfly nymphs you will notice leaflike gills. The **damselfly nymph** has three long ones at the tip of its abdomen (Fig. 2.16). The **mayfly nymph** has three long fila-

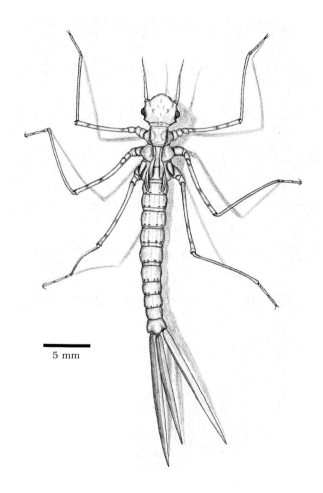

5 mm

2.16. BLACK-WINGED DAMSELFLY NYMPH.

ments that could pass for gills on superficial inspection, but they are used as feelers instead (Fig. 2.17). Its rapidly beating gills are arranged in seven pairs along its sides; the mayfly is the only aquatic nymph that can claim these features. Not only are the gills of the nymph shaped like leaves, but the many air tubes that radiate through each gill look just like the veins of a leaf.

2.17. MAYFLY NYMPH.

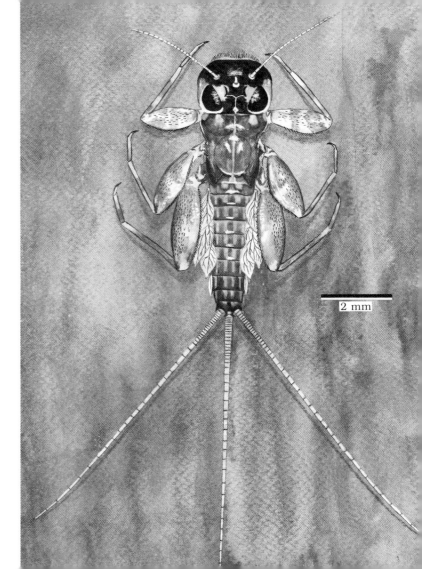

2 mm

Damselfly and **dragonfly nymphs** (Fig. 2.18) are but dim reflections of the winged adults that they will eventually become (see Figs. 2.30, 2.31). They rise from humble beginnings on bottom mud and develop into adults with large, intricately patterned wings and colors ranging from iridescent greens and blacks to delicate pastel blues and reds.

The forms and colors of the nymphs blend well with the landscape on the bottom of the pond and no doubt disguise them as they stalk prey to within reach of their most unusual lower lip called the labium (*labium*, lip). The labium is hinged and swings forward from the lower jaw just as a frog's well-aimed tongue springs forth from the floor of its mouth. It is the labium that snatches the prey and serves it to the waiting jaws.

At first glance, the dragonfly nymph presents a puzzling situation for an aquatic insect in which neither gills nor spiracles are evident. But if you watch a dragonfly nymph move about on the bottom of an aquarium, you will likely notice that it sometimes propels itself forward like a rocket. What it is actually doing is squirting water from its rectum. The dragonfly

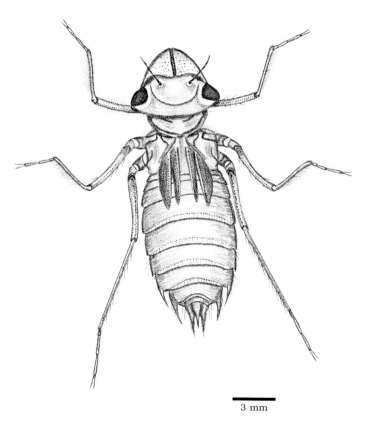

3 mm

2.18. DRAGONFLY NYMPH.

nymph constantly pumps water in and out of its rectum to breathe. The surface of the rectum is covered with a dense mat of air tubes (Fig. 2.19). Here, oxygen-depleted air is exchanged for oxygen-rich air that is dissolved in the water.

Place a drop of food coloring near the rectum of a nymph in a shallow pan of water; you will be able to see the water currents that are created by the nymph's breathing.

2.19. INSIDE VIEW OF A DRAGONFLY NYMPH.

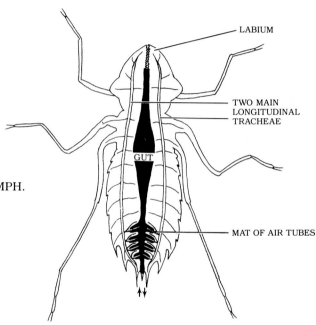

LABIUM

TWO MAIN
LONGITUDINAL
TRACHEAE

GUT

MAT OF AIR TUBES

2.20. ISOPOD.

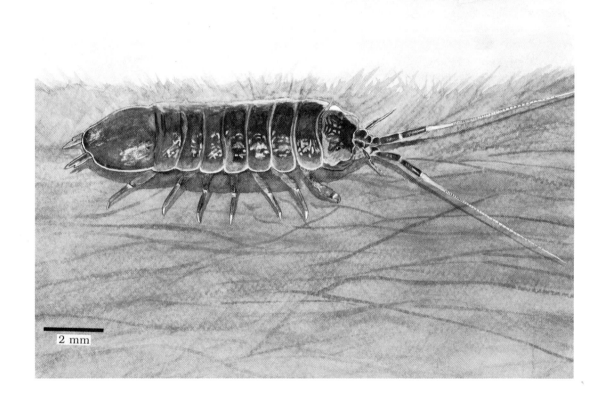

2 mm

Isopods and amphipods are the underwater versions of the wood louse (p. 146). You are very likely to come across them as you explore the weeds and muddy bottom of a pond. These crustaceans breathe with feathery gills, and like wood lice mothers, these mothers carry their eggs and newly hatched young in brood pouches on their abdomens. Flat, sluggish isopods (Fig. 2.20) generally plod along muddy bottoms and through thickets of algae, but the more agile amphipods (Fig. 2.21) seem to be endowed with exceptional acrobatic ability for they can jump, glide, and somersault like carefree children.

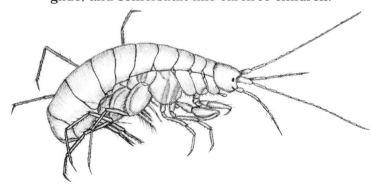

2.21.   AMPHIPOD.   1 mm

Skaters

NOT ONLY CAN insects and spiders walk on ceilings, but some of them can even walk on water. The forces that hold ice molecules together on the surface of a pond are strong enough to hold our weight during really cold weather. Similar attractive forces are present among water molecules on the pond's surface during the rest of the year, and they create a surface tension, which is like an elastic film that can support insects and spiders covered with nonwettable skeletons. Because molecules of water are repelled by the thousands of tiny hairs that cover the skeletons of these animals, the surface film is not broken; the weight of their feet only creates tiny dimples on the water's surface. However, those little creatures that are covered with wettable skeletons do not fare very well in their encounters with water. They break through the surface film and become hopelessly trapped by the attractive forces of water.

Some insects that live on the water surface span the interface between water and air. Their nonwettable parts are above the surface film;

their wettable parts are below the water film. As you will see, living on the "roof" of the pond and the "bottom" of the sky gives these creatures some peculiar attributes.

Water striders are the long-legged bugs that stalk the surfaces of calm waters (Fig. 2.22). On sunny days, their shadows create attractive designs on the bottoms of shallow pools. While skating over the water's film, the middle and hind legs of these striders stroke the surface, but the short front legs remain poised to grab any insects that may fall from the sky above or surface from the water below.

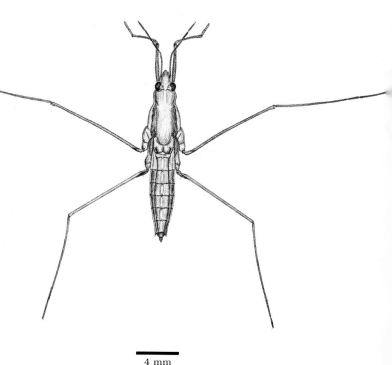

4 mm

2.22. WATER STRIDER.

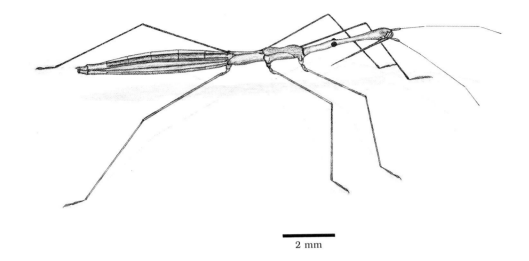

2 mm

Skinnier and considerably slower than the water striders, **water measurers** (Fig. 2.23) prefer the tangles of plants near shore to the open stretches of water frequented by the striders. Once you have watched one of these water measurers gingerly crossing stretches of water between weed stalks with its careful and delicate pacing, it will be obvious that its name was well chosen.

2.23.   WATER MEASURER.

47

After awakening from their winter slumber, **whirligig beetles** quickly join in the flurry of pond events that follows the winter thaw. They are a gregarious bunch and exuberantly whirl about on the surface film.

What seems so miraculous is that these beetles never seem to collide as they gyrate together. Long before humans discovered the principles of sonar for determining the positions of objects, whirligigs were using a similar method to determine the locations of their fellow beetles and other objects in contact with the water surface. Antennae of the whirligig float on the surface and monitor all ripples that pass their way (Fig. 2.24). With the information carried by these ripples, the beetle can make split-second decisions about the direction of its travels.

With one pair of eyes above water and another pair below, each beetle can simultaneously keep track of affairs above as well as below the water surface; this is the whirligig version of bifocal glasses. The eyes below the water have a different optical design from the eyes above the water.

The insects that live on the water surface receive and send ripples across the film—certainly a good way for these pond creatures to communicate. Try gently tapping the water with a stick or dropping a small object in the pond. The whirligigs and striders either will dash away or approach so you will get some idea what message—friend, foe, or food—your vibrations are sending to these insects.

2.24. WHIRLIGIG BEETLE.

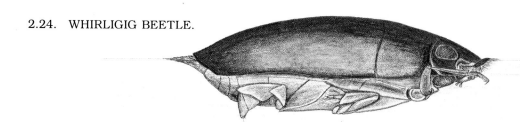

1 mm

Wrigglers

SOME AQUATIC INSECTS neither dive, crawl, nor skate. The larvae and pupae of certain midges and mosquitoes, for example, are better at wriggling than at any of these other means of water travel.

Midges (see Fig. 4.7) look a great deal like mosquitoes, but unlike mosquitoes, midges do not bite—at least not those whose larvae are mentioned here. The **phantom midge larva** is of such a glassy transparency that you would probably miss it when peering into a pond if it were not for two dark masses on each larva—one anterior and one posterior (Fig. 2.25). The dark objects are actually kidney-shaped air sacs into which oxygen moves by diffusion. The larva controls its depth by adjusting the air supply in the two main air sacs.

The larva has also found an unusual use for its hook-shaped antennae. Watch how it uses these antennae to grab the smaller pond animals on which it feeds.

2.25. PHANTOM MIDGE LARVA.

1 mm

2.26. BLOODWORM.

Down in the mud among the sticks and fallen leaves, lives a bright red wriggler. Some people call it a **bloodworm** (Fig. 2.26). The name is more appropriate than many realize, since the red color of the wriggler's blood is imparted by molecules of hemoglobin (*hemo,* blood; *globus,* ball) that are very similar to those we have in our own blood. Our hemoglobin combines with oxygen from the lungs and then distributes it throughout the body. Where this wriggler lives, oxygen is often in short supply, thus the hemoglobin molecules in its blood tightly bind oxygen that diffuses from the water through its thin cuticle. Insects and spiders often have green, yellow, or blue blood, but bloodworms are among the very few with red blood.

Biologists have given these midge larvae another name—chironomids. The Greek derivation of the word translates to "one who tells a story with movements of its body." After you have watched a larva wriggling about in the flimsy case it builds with a little silk and a little silt, you will understand why this name suits it very well.

Mosquito larvae maintain a foothold on the surface film with short siphons at their posterior ends (Fig. 2.27). The skin of the larvae is so transparent that the two air-filled tracheae are quite conspicuous along the backs of these wrigglers; both air tubes run through the siphon. A larva stocks up with air each time the nonwet-

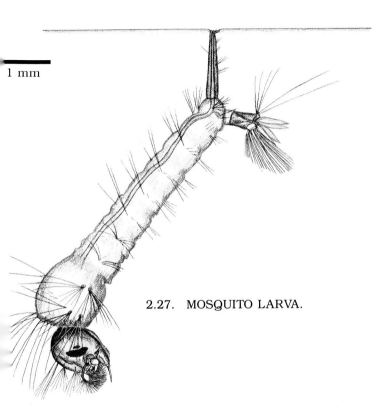

2.27.   MOSQUITO LARVA.

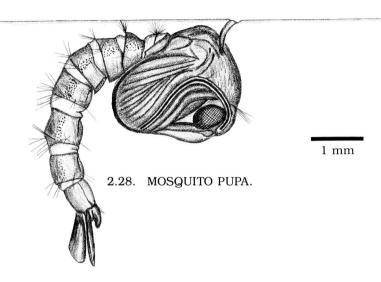

2.28.   MOSQUITO PUPA.

table end of its siphon breaks the surface film. Notice how a tap on the water surface sends the larva wriggling toward the bottom of the pond.

When the larva pupates and the adult mosquito begins forming within the pupal skeleton, the mosquito floats head up, rather than bottom up, and the siphon is now found on the top of the thorax rather than the tip of the abdomen (Fig. 2.28).

51

Patrollers of the Shore

THE WARTY **toad bugs** dwell on sand bars and muddy shores. Their family name—Gelastocoridae (*gelasto,* laughable; *coris,* bug)—tells us a lot about them. They look like tiny toads (Fig. 2.29), and their motley colors match the sandy backgrounds so well that sometimes only their hopping gives away their whereabouts. We can easily overlook these bugs on stretches of sand bars, and toad bugs are probably equally inconspicuous to their prey. With just one pounce, the toad bug usually acquires a meal.

The unobtrusive toad bugs often share the beach with flashy tiger beetles (p. 156). Two more different insect personalities are hard to imagine. While toad bugs lead reasonably unpretentious existences, tiger beetles dash about the shore with a great deal of bravado, swiftly overtaking prey on open stretches of the shore. They may take flight but quickly return to their beats along the shore.

2 mm

2.29. TOAD BUG.

52

2.30. DRAGONFLY SHARING PERCH WITH A NARROW-WINGED DAMSELFLY.

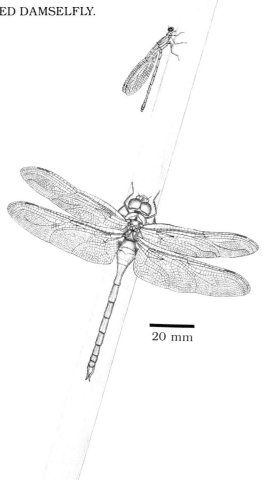

20 mm

The lives of **dragonflies** and **damselflies** have been intimately linked to the still waters of ponds, lakes, and swamps since their giant ancestors patrolled the skies over the coal swamps about 300 million years ago. Dragonflies glide resolutely along the shore, stopping every so often to survey their domains from favorite posts on bushes, reeds, or cattails (Fig. 2.30).

53

Damselflies (Fig. 2.31), however, flitter around ponds and streams, leading a slower-paced life than that of dragonflies. Their smaller wings and smaller wing muscles could never carry them over the banks of the pond with a speed comparable to that of the speedy dragonflies.

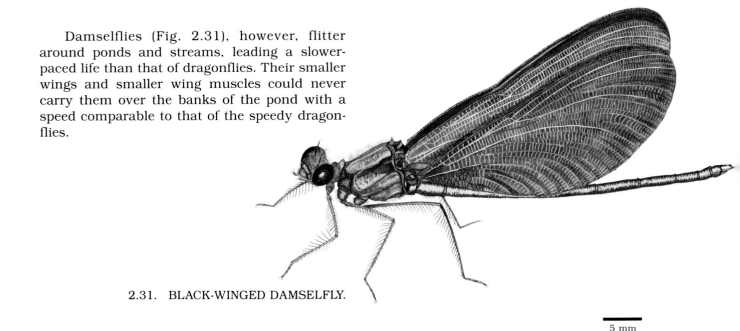

2.31.   BLACK-WINGED DAMSELFLY.

5 mm

If you examine the legs of either a damselfly or a dragonfly, you will see that each one is armed with two rows of long, sharp spines. With these spiny legs, they strain the air for mosquitoes, gnats, and midges as they cruise over the pond.

Once they alight on a reed or cattail, you will see that dragonflies hold their four long wings horizontally, but most damselflies hold their wings up and back. You will also notice that both of them have big, bulging eyes—the better to see mosquitoes with (Fig. 2.30, 2.31).

When you look into the eyes of a dragonfly or damselfly, you are looking into the eyes of a creature whose vision at close range may be as good as our own—and in some ways better.

The compound eyes of insects are collections of facets (Fig. 2.32A), each of which represents the surface of an ommatidium (*omma,* eye); the elements of each ommatidium correspond to a small simple eye. Ommatidia come in two main forms: those of insects active during the night (Fig. 2.32B) and those of insects active during the day (Fig. 2.32C).

2.32.   COMPOUND EYES OF DIURNAL AND NOCTURNAL INSECTS.

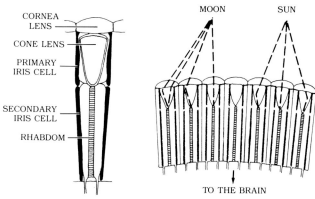

A. WEDGE OF FACETS FROM A COMPOUND EYE

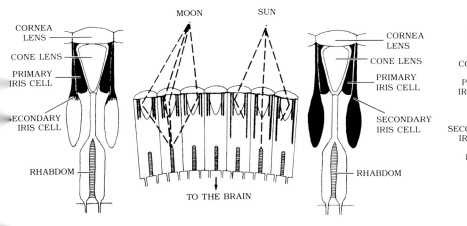

B. EYE OF NOCTURNAL INSECT

C. EYE OF DIURNAL INSECT

All ommatidia have certain features in common with each other and with our own eyes. The cornea lens and cone lens function like our own lens in focusing light on the region of the eye where light-sensitive molecules detect light and transmit this information to the brain. In our eyes this region is called the retina; in insects this region is called the rhabdom (*rhabdos,* rod). The dark, pigmented iris cells that lie along the side of each ommatidium serve the same purpose as our own irises (the part of our eyes that determines whether we have green, blue, or brown eyes). They control the amount of light that reaches the retina and rhabdom.

Figure 2.32(B, C) shows how the two different types of insect eyes process incoming light (dashed lines) from both the sun and the moon. In insects such as moths and fireflies that are active at night (nocturnal), each ommatidium receives moonlight not only through its own lens but also through adjacent lenses (Fig. 2.32B, moonlight), making the image much brighter than if each rhabdom collected light from only one ommatidium. Under the bright light of day, pigment granules in the secondary iris cells of these insects move down the side of each ommatidium; each ommatidium and each rhabdom of these night creatures now behave like those of day-flying (diurnal) insects such as dragonflies and butterflies (Fig. 2.32B, sunlight). Under sunlight as well as moonlight, each ommatidium in diurnal insects is completely surrounded by dark iris cells that prevent the light entering one ommatidium from reaching nearby ommatidia (Fig. 2.32C). Although the images of objects that these insects view under moonlight are much less bright than those viewed by nocturnal insects, the images are much sharper.

The greater the number of ommatidia, the more details an insect eye can pick out. Dragonflies and damselflies have between 10,000 and 28,000 ommatidia and have some of the sharpest eyesight. No wonder they are so good at spotting flying insects as well as people.

The precise organization of the insect eye and its connections with the brain are really quite astounding. Roman Vishniac, whose photographs celebrate the artistry of nature, was well aware of this order and design throughout the natural world: "Everything made by human hands looks terrible under magnification—crude, rough, and unsymmetrical. But in nature every bit of life is lovely. And the more magnification we use, the more details are brought out, perfectly formed, like endless sets of boxes within boxes."

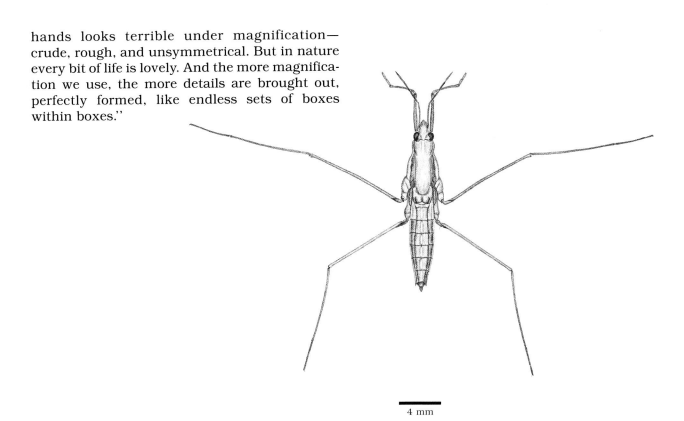

4 mm

CLASSIFICATION

Class Crustacea
    Fairy Shrimp
        Order Anostraca (*an*, without; *ostrakon*, shell)
            Family Chirocephalidae (*chiro*, hand; *cephalus*, head): **fairy shrimp**

    Isopods
        Order Isopoda (*isos*, equal; *poda*, feet)
            Family Asellidae (*asellus*, a kind of fish): **isopod**

    Amphipods
        Order Amphipoda (*amphi*, double; *poda*, feet)
            Family Gammaridae (*gammarus*, a kind of crab): **amphipod**

Class Insecta
    Stoneflies
        Order Plecoptera (*plectos*, plaited; *ptera*, wings)
            Family Perlidae (*perla*, a kind of insect): **stonefly** nymph

    Mayflies
        Order Ephemeroptera (*ephemeros*, lasting but a day; *ptera*, wings)
            Family Heptageniidae (*hepta*, seven; *genu*, joint): **mayfly** nymph

    Damselflies, Dragonflies
        Order Odonata (*odontos*, tooth)
            Family Coenagrionidae (*coeno*, common; *agrios*, living in the fields): **narrow-winged damselfly**
            Family Calopterygidae (*calo*, beautiful; *ptera*, wings): **black-winged damselfly** nymph and adult
            Family Aeshnidae (*aesch*, ugliness): **green darner dragonfly**
            Family Libellulidae (*libellula*, little balance): **dragonfly** nymph

True Bugs
    Order Hemiptera (*hemi*, half; *ptera*, wings)
        Family Notonectidae (*notos*, back; *nectes*, swimmer): **backswimmer**
        Family Corixidae (*coris*, a bug): **water boatman**
        Family Gerridae (*gerri*, wicker): **water strider**
        Family Hydrometridae (*hydro*, water; *metron*, measure): **water measurer**
        Family Gelastocoridae (*gelastos*, laughable; *coris*, bug): **toad bug**

Dobson Flies, Lacewings, Ant Lions
    Order Neuroptera (*neuron*, nerve; *ptera*, wings)
        Family Corydalidae (*corydalos*, crested lark): **dobson fly** larva

Caddis Flies
    Order Trichoptera (*trichos*, hair; *ptera*, wings)
        Family Brachycentridae (*brachys*, short; *centrum*, middle): **caddis fly** larva

True Flies
    Order Diptera (*dis*,two; *ptera*, wings)
        Family Chaoboridae (*chao*, empty; *bora*, meat): **phantom midge** larva
        Family Culicidae (*culex*, mosquito): **mosquito** larva and pupa
        Family Chironomidae (*chironomos*, one who tells a story with body movements): **bloodworm** (midge larva)

Beetles
    Order Coleoptera (*coleos*, sheath; *ptera*, wings)
        Family Dytiscidae (*dytes*, diver): **diving beetle** larva and adult
        Family Haliplidae (*halis*, abundant; *plos*, swimmer): **crawling water beetle**
        Family Psephanidae (*psephos*, pebble): **water penny beetle** larva
        Family Gyrinidae (*gyro*, turn around): **whirligig beetle**

3.1.

3. Meadows and Fields

MEADOWS AND FIELDS are home for creatures of amazing diversity. Predators and prey, plant feeders and animal feeders—all can exist within an area of a few square feet.

To give you some idea of the richness of life in a meadow, try gently sweeping an insect net through the grass, then flowers. Each sweep will collect a different assortment of insects and spiders. The combinations of creatures are seemingly endless, and even an entomologist would be hard-pressed to give you the exact names of each living form. Each glimpse into the bottom of the net is a glimpse into the kaleidoscope of spider and insect life.

61

Sap Suckers

JUST AS WE TAP maple trees for their sugar-rich sap in early spring, so many insects also tap stems and leaves for the same reason. For us, the syrup that we prepare from maple sap is a luxury, but for sap-sucking insects, the sap is a meal in itself. Since these insects can neither chew nor bite, plant juice is the only meal that they can consume with their piercing beaks.

—

The **aphid** and the **milkweed bug** are two of many insects that feed on sap from plants (Fig. 3.2). Sap-sucking insects have four mouthparts called stylets that can pierce leaves and stems. These four stylets are encased in a hollow beak (Fig. 3.3A). The two central stylets have matching grooves that form the food canal and the salivary canal (Fig. 3.3B). Saliva containing digestive juices passes down the salivary canal, and sap is pumped up the food canal into the gut. Muscles that stretch between the gut and the top of the head act as a sap pump by repeatedly contracting and relaxing.

62

3.2.   SAP-SUCKING INSECTS OF MILKWEED.

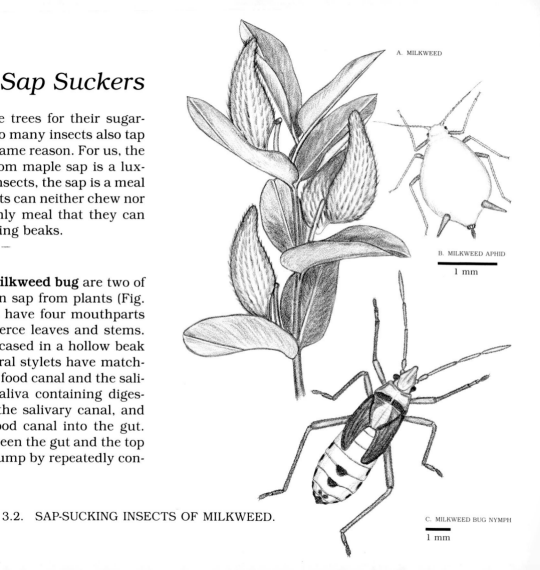

A. MILKWEED

B. MILKWEED APHID

1 mm

C. MILKWEED BUG NYMPH

1 mm

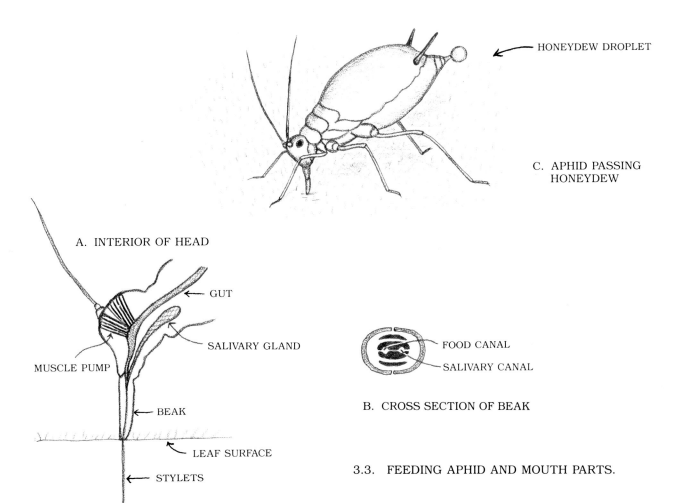

HONEYDEW DROPLET

C. APHID PASSING
HONEYDEW

A. INTERIOR OF HEAD

GUT

SALIVARY GLAND

MUSCLE PUMP

FOOD CANAL

SALIVARY CANAL

B. CROSS SECTION OF BEAK

BEAK

LEAF SURFACE

STYLETS

3.3. FEEDING APHID AND MOUTH PARTS.

63

Aphids are found on trees, flowers, and weeds, and where you find one, you are very likely to find many more. Like their close relatives the treehoppers (p. 65), aphids use only a portion of the sugars found in the sap that they suck from a plant. The unused and concentrated sugars are passed through the gut in the form of honeydew droplets (Fig. 3.3C). Ants seem to be as fond of aphid honeydew as they are of treehopper honeydew, so you are very likely to find ants wherever you find an aphid colony.

Pick a stalk or stem that is covered with aphids. Place the cut end of the plant in a small bottle of water and then plug the mouth of the bottle with a wad of cotton or paper toweling (Fig. 3.4). Any number of containers can serve as observation cages for the aphids—a large jar, a terrarium, a clear plastic box. As long as you are gentle, the aphids and their companions should continue about their affairs for many hours.

Who would suspect that little aphids lead very complex lives? The first aphids of the year hatch from eggs that were laid the preceding fall. Everyone of these aphids is a female, and everyone is wingless. They neither mate nor lay eggs, but they conceive without males by a process

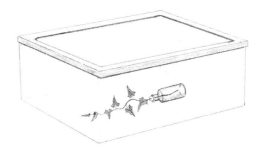

known as parthenogenesis (*parthenos*, virgin; *genesis*, birth), giving birth to live young. All these young are wingless females like their mothers. A new generation of wingless females can appear as often as every 10 days until the leaves and stems on which they feed become too crowded. Wingless mothers then give birth to winged daughters that fly off to colonize new leaves and stems. These winged generations can alternate with wingless generations several times during the course of the summer until the final generation of aphids (the 12th or 13th!) appears. At last, male aphids make their appearance and mate with the females; the year ends as it began with the fertilized eggs that they leave behind.

Treehoppers are often sociable creatures, and mother treehoppers remain with their children long after they hatch. Not only are treehoppers found in the company of their own kind, but they are also frequent companions of ants. Treehoppers sip on plant juices, and the ants await their share of the feast—the sweet droppings of honeydew. At the treehopper banquet, the ants are far from being unwelcome guests; they act as nursemaids and protect their charges from predators (Fig. 3.5). With her brood under the watchful eyes of the ants, a mother treehopper may move on to another leaf to lay more eggs. Without help from the ants, she would probably manage only a single brood at any given time. All in all, it is a good relationship for both the treehoppers and the ants.

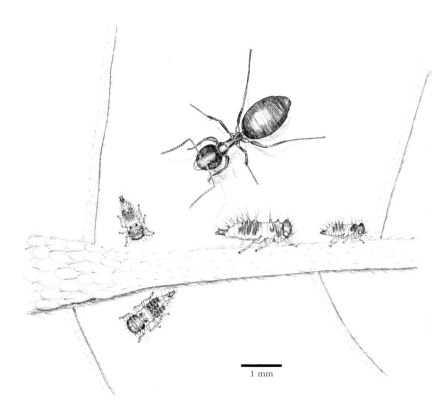

1 mm

3.5.   TREEHOPPER NYMPHS AND EGGS (*left*) ATTENDED BY AN ANT.

Weevils are known for their long snouts, katydids for their long antennae, but no other group of insects has a single segment of its body sculptured in the diverse and often outlandish style of the treehoppers. Spines, horns, pits, ridges, humps, and bumps—any of these can appear on the segment between the head and wings of adult treehoppers (Fig. 3.6). Some treehoppers look as though they are thorns sprouting from a branch; others look more like ornate and abstract sculpture.

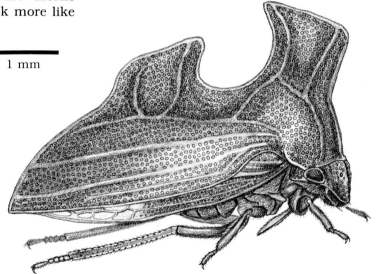

1 mm

3.6. TREEHOPPER ADULT.

3.7. LEAFHOPPER.

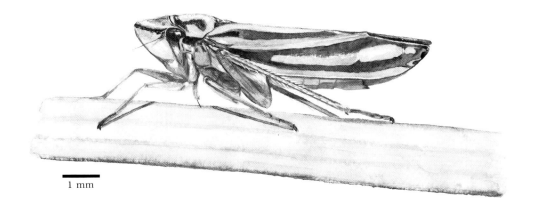

1 mm

A sweep of a butterfly net through the plants of a meadow usually yields a variety of stream-lined **leafhoppers** (Fig. 3.7). For the most part, they will be green, but some species are brightly spotted or striped.

Leafhoppers spend their days sipping sap and squirting drops of honeydew. When a leafhopper finds a good source of sap, it can fire several drops of honeydew each minute. In parts of the United States this talent has earned them the other name of "sharpshooters." At night they flock by the thousands to any nearby lights. And, of course, there are always those that, like Icarus of the Greek myth, venture too close, only to scorch their wings and plummet to the earth.

Although the **spittle bug** itself is hidden from view, its whereabouts are betrayed by its frothy quarters (Fig. 3.8). The view from the interior of this house of bubbles must be kaleidoscopic, as light is probably split, bent, dispersed, and generally tossed about within the froth.

At the core of the froth, the spittle bug sips on plant juice. After passing through the spittle bug, the juice serves as a useful building material, but only if whipped to the right consistency; plant juice alone could never be whipped into a stiff froth. The secret to the consistency of the froth lies in a protein thickener that is added to the juice in the gut of the spittle bug (Fig. 3.9). This thickener is produced by long strands of tissue known as Malpighian tubes. The tubes were named after the Italian scientist Marcello Malpighi who first described them in a caterpillar in 1669. The principal function of these tubes is to absorb wastes from the blood of an insect in much the same fashion as kidneys in larger animals, but in spittle bugs, the tubes have taken on this additional chore of protein secretion. These proteins make the foam sturdy, like a stiff meringue whipped from the proteins of egg whites.

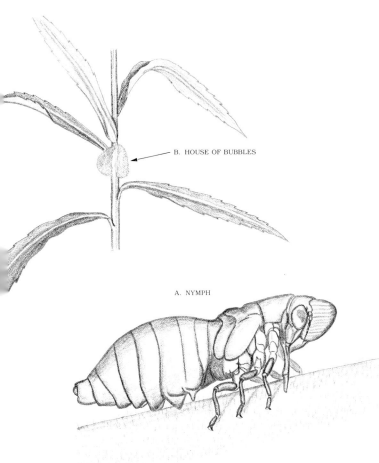

B. HOUSE OF BUBBLES

A. NYMPH

1 mm

3.8. SPITTLE BUG.

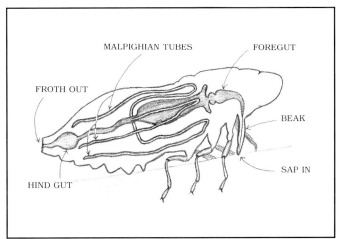

MALPIGHIAN TUBES

FOREGUT

FROTH OUT

BEAK

HIND GUT

SAP IN

3.9. INSIDE VIEW OF GUT AND MALPIGHIAN TUBES IN A SPITTLE BUG.

Nectar Sippers

INSECTS HAVE DINED on plants for millions of years, yet the plants have endured. To discourage hungry trespassers, many plants have tainted their leaves and stems with distasteful chemicals or coated their surfaces with spines or sticky hairs.

Plants such as goldenrod, however, have succeeded best at cooperation rather than at confrontation with insects (Fig. 3.10). Ever since flowering plants first appeared during the age of the dinosaurs, they have enticed insects with their tasty gifts of nectar and pollen, and insects have repaid the flowers by carrying their pollen from plant to plant. The many and beautiful forms of both flowers and insects have been molded by this remarkable partnership.

Although bristly **tachinid flies** (Fig. 3.11) spend most of their hours lapping nectar from flowers, tachinid larvae reside as uninvited

3.10. GOLDENROD.

70

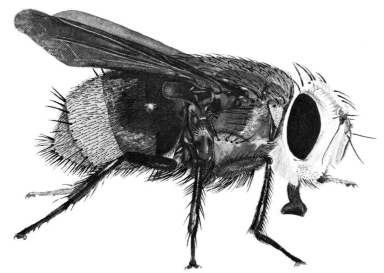

3.11.   TACHINID FLY.

1 mm

guests (parasites) inside other insects, living at the expense of their hosts. Leading such a life can be demanding for both parasite and host. The mother tachinid is responsible for locating a suitable home for her children. Home can be a caterpillar, grub, beetle, grasshopper, or any number of other insects; each species of fly usually has a favorite host and a favorite method for finding it. Many flies will place their eggs on a leaf where they, along with the leaf, are likely to be swallowed by the hungry insect host. Only after an egg has been swallowed will the fly maggot hatch and take up residence in its host. Other flies, however, will first locate a host and then place their eggs directly on the victim, and then still others simply scatter hundreds of eggs in places frequented by appropriate hosts; at least a few of their larvae will find a home to their liking.

3.12. PAINTED LADY BUTTERFLY ON A THISTLE FLOWER.

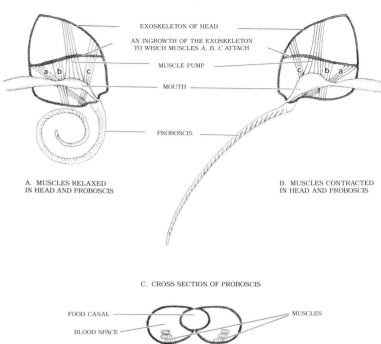

EXOSKELETON OF HEAD

AN INGROWTH OF THE EXOSKELETON TO WHICH MUSCLES A. B. C ATTACH

MUSCLE PUMP

MOUTH

PROBOSCIS

A. MUSCLES RELAXED IN HEAD AND PROBOSCIS

B. MUSCLES CONTRACTED IN HEAD AND PROBOSCIS

C. CROSS SECTION OF PROBOSCIS

FOOD CANAL

MUSCLES

BLOOD SPACE

3.13. HEAD AND PROBOSCIS OF A BUTTERFLY.

Nectar sipping is an old profession for insects. Bees, flies, and bugs that sip nectar from flowers all have modified mouthparts rolled into sucking tubes. The sucking tubes of butterflies and moths, however, are by far the longest and can reach deep into even the largest flowers for the sweet stores of nectar (Fig. 3.12).

The "tongues" of moths and butterflies are so long, in fact, that they remain coiled up when not in use (Fig. 3.13A). The tongue (or proboscis) uncoils in the same way that a toy paper snake unfurls when you blow on it. The air from your lungs extends the paper snake. A butterfly extends its proboscis by inflating it with blood from its head. When the muscles in its head contract, the blood space in the head shrinks, and blood is

squeezed into the proboscis. At the same time, tiny muscles in the proboscis, shown as oblique lines, also contract and flatten the curved upper surface of the proboscis (Fig. 3.13B).

72

A cross section of the butterfly proboscis shows that two mouthparts zipper together along their inner surfaces to form a food canal for nectar (Fig. 3.13C).

When a fly sticks out its tongue to lap up nectar, both blood and air inflate the tongue (Fig. 3.14). Grooves on the bottom of the tongue channel nectar to the center of the proboscis where the mouth is located. From there it is pumped into the gut by repeated contraction and relaxation of the muscle pump in the head. The pump in the head of a butterfly works in similar fashion.

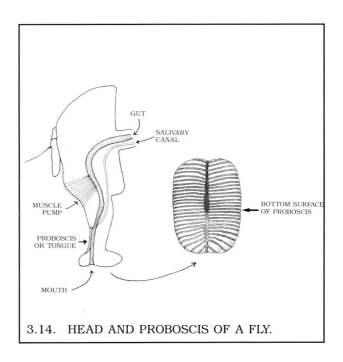

3.14. HEAD AND PROBOSCIS OF A FLY.

73

Do not be surprised if on first encounter you mistake the rotund **negro bug** (Fig. 3.15) for a beetle. Its wing covers are not parted down the middle of its back as they would be if it really were a beetle. Inspection of the ventral surface also reveals a mouth suited for sucking, not for chewing. No beetle has a mouth like this.

Negro bugs not only seek the nectar of goldenrod, but they also seem particularly fond of the large flowerheads of Queen Anne's lace and wild parsnip that dot pastures and fence-rows during the hottest days of summer. On the white and yellow lace of these flowers, they glisten like pebbles of burnished obsidian (volcanic glass).

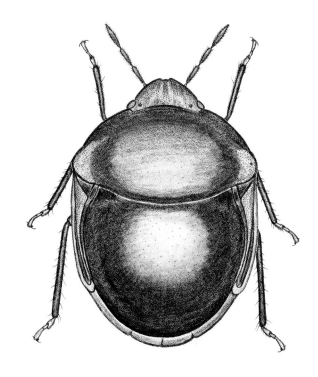

3.15. NEGRO BUG.

1 mm

From their buzzing and their colors, **syrphid flies** are often mistaken for bees or wasps. Although this masquerade makes them seem tough, they can neither sting nor bite. There is no need to worry if one should land on your arm and begin lapping up sweat.

To some people, syrphids are also known as **hover flies** (Fig. 3.16). After you have watched one for a few minutes, the reason for the name will be obvious. Darting from flower to flower, a syrphid may suddenly hover on rapidly beating wings and then abruptly disappear, only to materialize at another spot nearby.

While adult syrphids seek the companionship of flowers, larval syrphids keep company with many different species of arthropods. Some lodge in rotten logs, others in shallow, stagnant pools. A few species are accepted as scavengers in ant and bee colonies. When you find a family of aphids on a leaf or stem, in their midst you may see a syrphid larva—a pale green maggot, not gathering honeydew but picking off aphids, one by one.

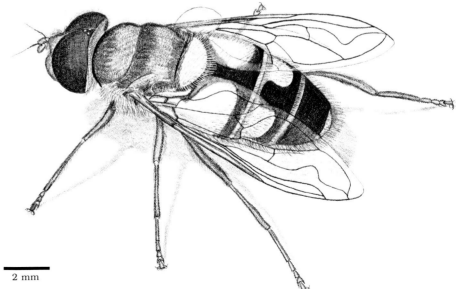

3.16. HOVER FLY.

2 mm

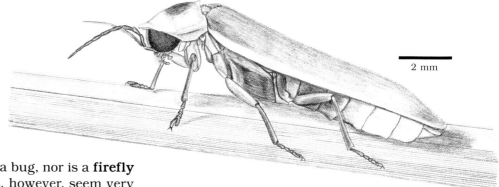

3.17. FIREFLY.

2 mm

A **lightning bug** is not a bug, nor is a **firefly** a fly. These popular names, however, seem very fitting for the beetle whose magical qualities have inspired so much of our poetry and prose (Fig. 3.17).

Lightning bugs or fireflies go courting on midsummer nights. With different species of fireflies courting in the same field, fireflies could get their courting signals crossed if each species did not have its own flashing code; however, females of one species can flash the code of another species. They flash from the ground and wait for a hovering male of the other species to be charmed with their display. Once they have his attention, they use their charms to entice him, not for romantic purposes, but for dinner instead.

Many tiny air tubes called tracheoles permeate the posterior end of the firefly, supplying molecules of oxygen that combine with other molecules produced by the cells in the light-producing tissue. Like a lighted firecracker, this complex of molecules is very unstable. However, when a firecracker goes off, energy is released in the form of light, heat, and noise, but when the complex of molecules in the firefly's tail breaks down, the energy it releases is almost entirely in the form of light (Fig. 3.18). Unlike a light bulb, firefly lights never get hot, or even warm.

You do not have to worry about your fingers getting hot from collecting fireflies, but you do have to worry about fireflies surviving in captivity. Watch those that you catch for only a few minutes and then release them. If they linger in a jar, they will soon lose the regular rhythm of their flashes, and their lights will slowly fade.

3.18.　EVENING DISPLAY BY FIREFLIES.

77

The **soldier beetle** is a close relative of the firefly (Fig. 3.19). Both these beetles are covered with a soft, pliable cuticle—certainly not the best protection at times. But then feeding on the nectar and pollen of goldenrod does not expose these beetles to very harsh and demanding conditions. They cover the flowers in such numbers that these black and orange beetles may well be the most abundant residents of the goldenrod community.

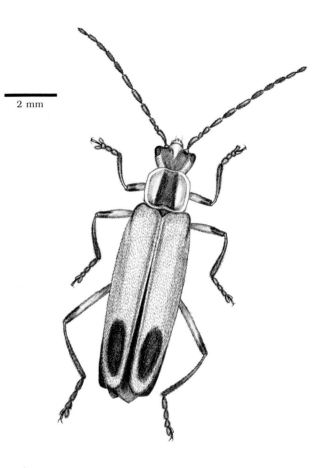

2 mm

3.19.   SOLDIER BEETLE.

Probably no other insect has had more articles and books written about it than the **honey bee,** but after all, the honey bee is really a remarkable creature (Fig. 3.20). Honey bees have existed in the company of humans for centuries as suppliers of honey and as pollinators of our crops. With the exception of the silk moth, the honey bee is the only insect that has ever been truly domesticated. Honey bees are also social insects and live in large communities with as many as 50,000 bees. Rigid social rules maintain order in a honey bee society: only one female in each colony (the queen) lays eggs; only sterile females (workers) collect the nectar and pollen, rear the young, and do the housekeeping; the males (drones) never help with the work but only mate with the queens. Honey bees even have special dances that the workers perform to relay information of great importance to them—where to find nectar and pollen.

The female workers of the bee colony do practically everything. They gather pollen and nectar, prepare honey and bee bread, construct honeycombs from wax produced by glands on their abdomens, feed the larval bees, and fan the hive with their wings on hot summer days. The

3.20. WORKER HONEY BEE.

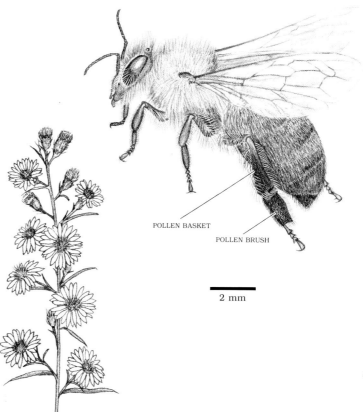

POLLEN BASKET

POLLEN BRUSH

2 mm

79

honey is nectar that is first partially digested and then regurgitated. When honey is mixed with pollen, it makes a nutritious paste called bee bread, which is fed to the larvae.

The only job the drones perform for the hive is fertilizing the eggs of the queen. Female larvae hatch from these fertilized eggs; most will become workers, and only a select few will become queens. The potential queens are the larvae that are fed the "royal jelly," a richer blend of honey and pollen than the regular bee bread fed to the other larvae. Ironically, drones only develop from eggs that are not fertilized by other drones.

The next time you see a worker bee going about its business, take a closer look at what it is doing. It will probably be too preoccupied with gathering pollen and nectar to notice you.

Pollen sticks to the many hairs that cover the honey bee. After each good dusting with pollen, the bee grooms itself with a leg brush and then deposits the pollen in baskets on its hind legs. When these baskets are filled to capacity with yellow pollen, the worker returns to the hubbub of the hive.

By setting up a glass-covered observation hive, you can watch the workings within this insect city and observe the unique ways of the honey bee—its wax making and honey making, its dances and social interactions. Information about suppliers of honey bees and observation hives will get you started (see Appendix).

Hunters and Stalkers

LIKE THE WILDEBEEST and zebra of the African Serengeti, the sap suckers, leaf grazers, and gatherers of pollen and nectar must always keep a sharp lookout for hunters and stalkers lying in ambush. The appetites of these predators keep the populations of prolific plant eaters from ballooning to astronomic levels and help to establish a delicate balance among plant and animal life.

Our own attempts to control certain plant-eating insects so often work against this balance and create new, and even worse, problems. Our numerous experiences using chemicals to control insects present many sad examples of human technology gone astray. Let us hope that our failures may at least instill in us some modesty about our technology and a healthier respect for the forces of nature. After all, as the ecologist Paul Errington described them thirty years ago, they are "forces that are much older, much more permanent, and much mightier than man."

From her perch atop a blackberry bush, this **praying mantis** surveys her portion of the meadow (Fig. 3.21). She spends the entire summer feeding and growing, and come September, she will mate and leave her frothy case of eggs on a blackberry stem.

You are likely to come across one of these egg cases on a winter walk through the meadow (Fig. 3.22). If you bring it home, leave it outdoors until the first warm days of spring—you do not want the mantises to hatch in the middle of winter before they can find other insects on which to feed. Baby mantises hatch with a good appetite and will devour whatever insects they come across, including their brothers and sisters. Rather than trying to raise mantises in a terrarium, even a large one, you will probably be more successful if

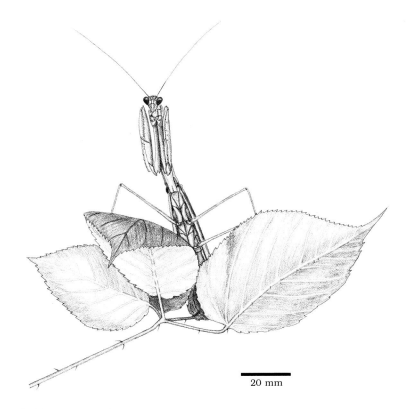

20 mm

3.21. PRAYING MANTIS.

10 mm

3.22.
PRAYING
MANTIS
EGG
CASE.

you place the egg case in a nearby bush or patch of weeds with its own community of flies, bugs, and other prey for the mantises to feed on.

Visit the bush or weeds periodically and you will probably find one or more members of the mantis brood. Their green bodies blend so well with leaves and stems, however, that you might have a hard time finding them, especially while they are still small. Once found, mantises stand their ground and will often accept small chunks of meat or fruit that are offered to them from the tip of a toothpick. You might also try offering them water from a teaspoon. After watching these graceful insects, poised for ambush or looking over their shoulders, you will understand the special appeal they have had to people of many cultures.

From an aphid's viewpoint, the **ladybird beetle** is far from being the gentle creature that we depict it as being. Ladybirds of all ages have a craving for aphids; larval ladybirds (Fig. 3.23) have even bigger appetites than do the adults (Fig. 3.24). After a summer of solitary feasting, adults congregate by the hundreds, thousands, or even millions to overwinter in some sheltered spot until spring brings forth another generation of aphids.

While ladybirds may be the aggressors to aphids, they must also deal with their own aggressors. Threatening situations such as curious fingers and curious beaks can literally raise the blood pressure of a ladybird. At its leg joints, which are the points of least resistance to the pressure, yellow, foul-smelling blood oozes forth to leave an unpleasant reminder with anyone who annoys the ladybird.

3.23. LADYBIRD BEETLE LARVA.

3.24. LADYBIRD BEETLE ADULT.

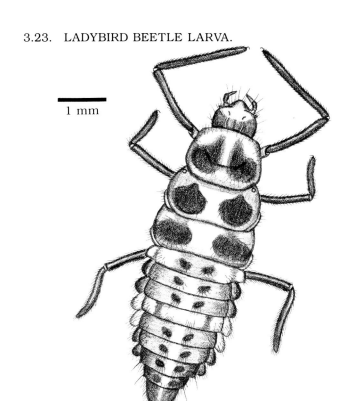

1 mm

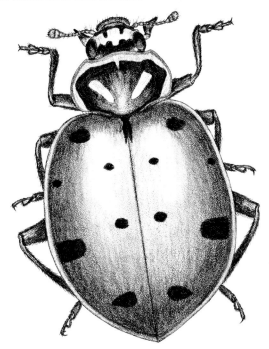

1 mm

83

The spiny **aphid lion** (Fig. 3.25) and the **golden-eyed lacewing** are unlikely relatives. The lacewing silently flies on gossamer wings; its larvae, the aphid lions, prowl among flocks of aphids, dispatching each one within a minute or less. In shape and color, these larvae and the lacewing seem worlds apart; but in their fondness for aphids, they share a definite kinship.

The sickle-shaped jaws of the larva are hollow like straws, and once they impale an aphid, they quickly drain it dry. Each jaw really consists of two parts that interlock to form a hollow tube (Fig. 3.26).

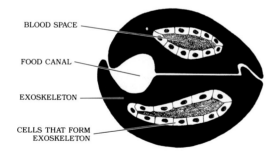

3.26.   CROSS SECTION OF JAW OF AN APHID LION.

84

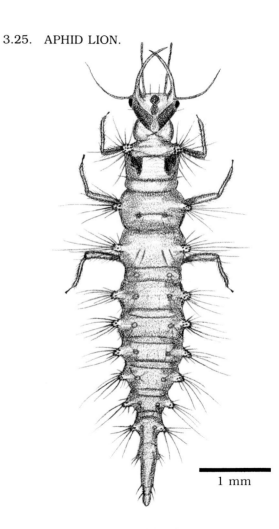

3.25.   APHID LION.

1 mm

After it has gorged on aphids for about 2 weeks, the aphid lion spins a silk cocoon in which it will retire for about another 2 weeks. Its energy will no longer be devoted to aphid hunting but strictly to the breakdown of its old, larval form and the unfolding of its new adult form, the golden-eyed lacewing (Fig. 3.27).

The adults are creatures of the twilight and evening hours. They may move placidly in the sunlight, but as twilight approaches, their activity accelerates. As though timed by a clock, feeding, mating, and egg laying are scheduled primarily for only certain hours of the day. This seemingly defenseless and fragile creature appears particularly vulnerable as it busies itself with these tasks. You will discover, however, if you get close enough, that the lacewing is blessed with a foul and penetrating odor. Nature rarely bestows innocence without power.

3.27. GOLDEN-EYED LACEWING.

2 mm

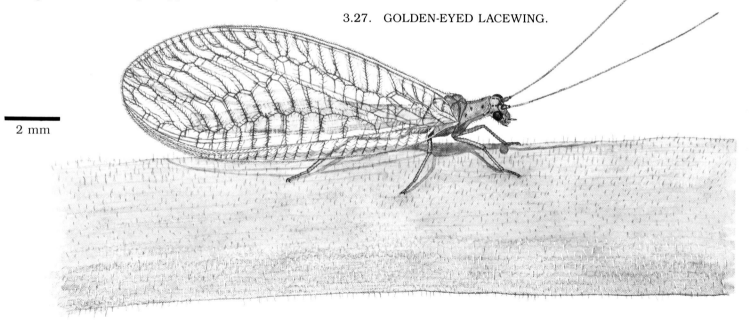

Jumping spiders (Fig. 3.28) have a fondness for sunny places where their colors are seen to best advantage. An observant eye can rarely mistake the sudden, jerky hops of jumping spiders. With their bright, often iridescent, colors and large eyes, they are considered among the most handsome and keenest-eyed spiders.

Jumping spiders seem to be aware of their good looks and rather flaunt them in their courtship dance. These spiders have perfected a dance routine in which the male leads by hopping toward the female and waving his legs and abdomen (Fig. 3.29). She, if suitably impressed, responds to her partner's advances by hopping and signaling with her legs. This dance can go on for many minutes until the romantic encounter ends with an embrace—but sometimes a rejection. The males are apparently great flirts, for you often find them performing for lady spiders.

3.28. JUMPING SPIDER.

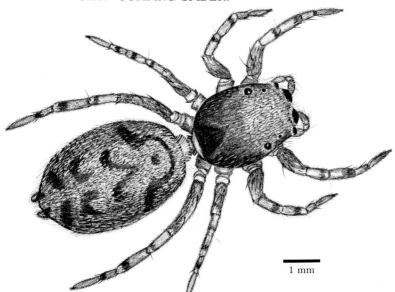

1 mm

3.29. JUMPING SPIDER IN MATING DANCE.

1 mm

Long-legged flies are tiny but conspicuous hunters of the meadow and brookside (Fig. 3.30).

3.30.   LONG-LEGGED FLY.

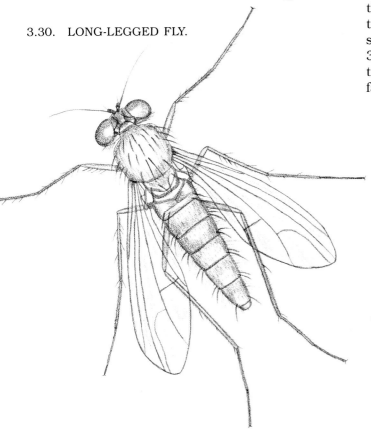

1 mm

While most insects attempt to remain concealed, long-legged flies are unabashed about exhibiting their finery. Ostentation seems to come naturally to these iridescent green and orange flies. They strut briskly over the surfaces of leaves (Fig. 3.31), constantly pausing to rub their hind legs together or to stroke them against the lower surfaces of their wings.

3.31.   LONG-LEGGED FLY ON A LEAF.

Stink bugs come in one general shape, but in many colors and with many habits (Fig. 3.32). Stink bugs can be brown, black, green, orange, or combinations of these colors. Their shield-shaped forms and telling odors make this group of bugs almost unmistakable. Stink bugs such as this one happen to prey on other insects found in meadows, but many species prefer vegetable juices to insect juices.

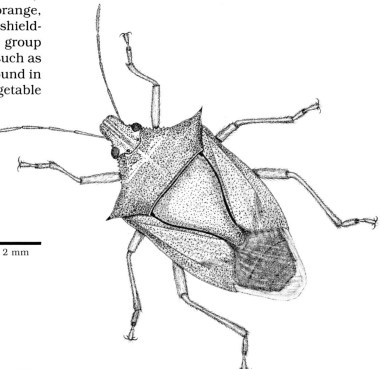

2 mm

3.32. STINK BUG.

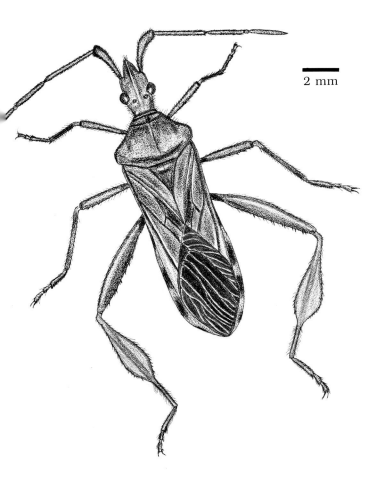

2 mm

While **leaf-footed bugs** (Fig. 3.33) busy themselves with preying on other insects, they keep a wary eye out for passing tachinid flies and hungry birds. These bugs, however, can smell as foul as any stink bug. A good whiff of one could cause even a famished bird to forget the urgings of an empty stomach. If it were not for the distinctive shape of those hind legs, the name stink bug might well have been assigned to this insect.

If you catch a leaf-footed bug or a stink bug in the middle of its dinner, you will notice that it feeds just as aphids, treehoppers, and spittle-bugs do—with a long, piercing beak.

3.33.   LEAF-FOOTED BUG.

89

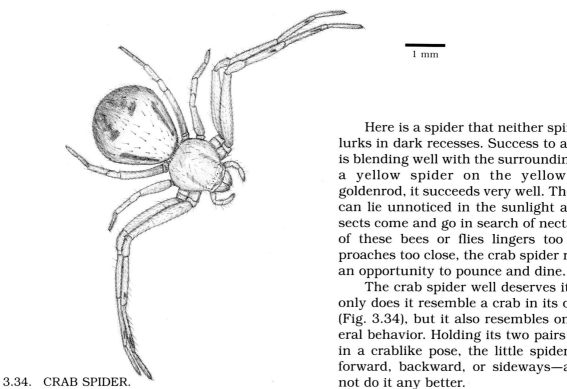

1 mm

Here is a spider that neither spins a web nor lurks in dark recesses. Success to a **crab spider** is blending well with the surrounding flowers; as a yellow spider on the yellow flowers of goldenrod, it succeeds very well. The crab spider can lie unnoticed in the sunlight as winged insects come and go in search of nectar, but if one of these bees or flies lingers too long or approaches too close, the crab spider rarely misses an opportunity to pounce and dine.

The crab spider well deserves its name. Not only does it resemble a crab in its overall shape (Fig. 3.34), but it also resembles one in its general behavior. Holding its two pairs of front legs in a crablike pose, the little spider can scuttle forward, backward, or sideways—a crab could not do it any better.

3.34.   CRAB SPIDER.

Wherever there is a crab spider on a goldenrod flower, there is very likely to be an **ambush bug** lurking nearby (Fig. 3.35). These bugs do just what their name implies—they ambush unsuspecting creatures that come in search of the stores of goldenrod nectar and pollen. Although less than an inch long and not particularly speedy, the ambush bug is able to surprise and overpower insects as large as bumble bees. Among the stocks-in-trade of the ambush bug are its powerful front legs and its camouflage. The mosaic arrangement of green, yellow, and brown pigments on its body blends well with the pattern of the goldenrod flower.

Probably the easiest way to find an ambush bug or a crab spider on a flower is to look for the stiff and lifeless forms of flies, bees, and even butterflies. At the other end of these lifeless insects, you will very likely find a dining spider or a dining bug.

2 mm

3.35.   AMBUSH BUG.

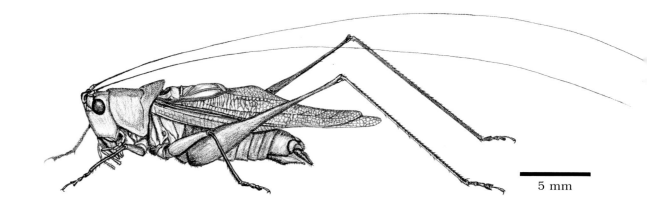

5 mm

Musicians of the Meadow

GRASSHOPPERS, katydids, and crickets are a vocal bunch, but these musicians really do not get warmed up until late summer. Like their close kin, the mantises and walkingsticks, these insects do not reach their full size until this time; only then, in their days of maturity, do the males acquire suitable instrumentation for their familiar serenades.

3.36. LONG-HORNED GRASSHOPPER.

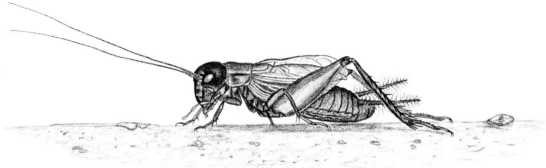

5 mm

Long-horned grasshoppers (Fig. 3.36), as well as katydids and crickets, fiddle by rubbing a corrugated patch or file on the under surface of one wing against a rough patch (scraper) on the upper surface of the other wing. In some species, the file is on the left wing, and the males are left-handed musicians. In other species, the file is on the right wing, and then the musicians are right-handed, like the **cricket** in Figure 3.37.

The music created by these files and scrapers varies from "zeep-zeep-zeep," "zip-zip-zip," and "katydid–katydidn't" of the long-horned grasshoppers to the "chirp-chirp" and "retreat, retreat" of the crickets.

93

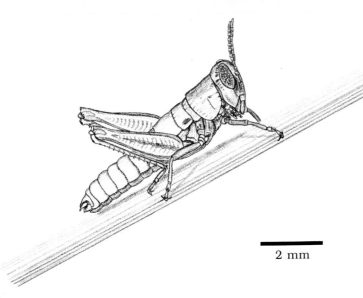

2 mm

and long-horned grasshoppers, ears are located on their front legs; in short-horned grasshoppers, the ears are found even further from the head, on the first segment of the abdomen. Crickets and katydids have ears near their knees (Fig. 3.39A, C, arrows). A cross section of each ear (Fig. 3.39B, D) shows that even though it is located on the leg, an insect ear is built very much like one of our own ears. Each has eardrums (*d*) and each has special cells (arrowheads) that detect the vibrations of the eardrums and transmit this information on sound to the ganglia and brain. The large chambers (*T*) are air tubes that pass through the legs, the gray area is space for blood, and black areas are the exoskeleton. There are tiny cells on the inner surface of the exoskeleton that are responsible for its formation.

With some chunks of apple or potato, a few bits of dry dog food, and a small carton in which to retire, crickets can readily adjust to life in a terrarium or large plastic box. The males will chirp and occasionally get into fights with each other, while the females will spend a good por-

Short-horned grasshoppers (Fig. 3.38) use a row of tiny pegs on the inside surface of their hind legs as bows for scratching and scraping the rough surface of their folded wings. You can feel these pegs on a full-grown grasshopper by gently rubbing your finger across the inner surface of its leg. The rasping sound they produce does not sound very musical to our ears, but after all, we all have different ears for music.

You see, this music of the fiddlers falls on receptive, but oddly placed, insect ears. In crickets

3.39. CRICKET AND KATYDID LEGS SHOWING EARDRUMS (d), AIR TUBES (T), AND SPECIAL CELLS (◄) OF THE EAR.

tion of their time laying eggs if you provide them with a shallow dish of damp sand or soil. Their strong and sharp ovipositors (*ovum*, egg; *positus*, deposited) move in and out of the soil with ease. Within a week after egg laying, there should be many tiny, flealike crickets hopping about.

If you have a friend who also has crickets, you might try an experiment in cricket communications. Listen to your friend's crickets over the telephone, and see if their chirps sound the same after passing through the telephone lines. Then let your crickets listen to each other and see how they respond to telephone messages.

Listening to the sound of cricket music can be a soothing experience, but it can also be utilitarian. The number of chirps per minute can tell us with great reliability how warm or how cold it is. Listen to your local weather report, and then listen to the crickets outside. After doing this several times, you will appreciate the trustworthiness of the cricket thermometer.

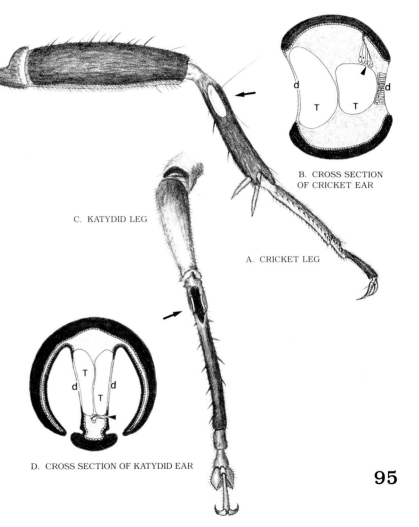

B. CROSS SECTION OF CRICKET EAR

C. KATYDID LEG

A. CRICKET LEG

D. CROSS SECTION OF KATYDID EAR

95

3.40. CICADA.

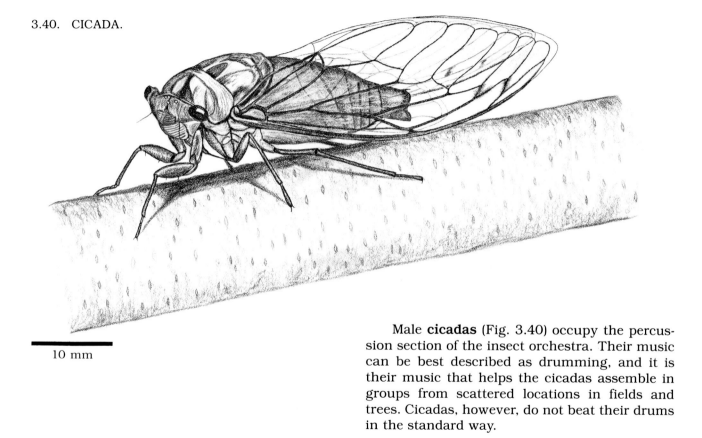

10 mm

Male **cicadas** (Fig. 3.40) occupy the percussion section of the insect orchestra. Their music can be best described as drumming, and it is their music that helps the cicadas assemble in groups from scattered locations in fields and trees. Cicadas, however, do not beat their drums in the standard way.

Let us take a look inside the cicada to see what makes its drums so different. The cicada's musical appartus is in the mid-region under two large flaps called opercula (*operculum,* cover) (Fig. 3.41A: *o*). Looking at a cross section through the region (Fig. 3.41B), you see that the drums (*d*) are part of the exoskeleton and stiff like most of the exoskeleton. When the powerful muscles (*M*) attached to each of the drums contract, the drums buckle inward. As soon as the muscles relax, the drums snap back to their original shape. The sides of an empty soda can behave in the same way when you push them in and then let them snap back. Although a soda can does not sound very much like a cicada, you need to realize that the muscles attached to the drums can contract and relax almost 400 times per second. In addition, the sound of the drums echoes through the air chambers of the body and is further amplified and enriched by thin and shiny membranes (*m*) that look like mirrors.

3.41. DRUMMING APPARATUS OF THE CICADA.

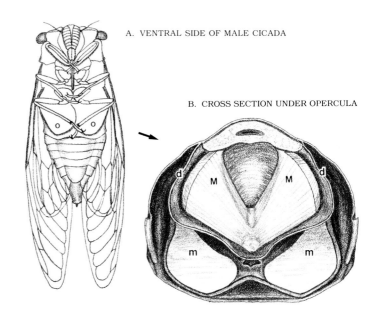

A. VENTRAL SIDE OF MALE CICADA

B. CROSS SECTION UNDER OPERCULA

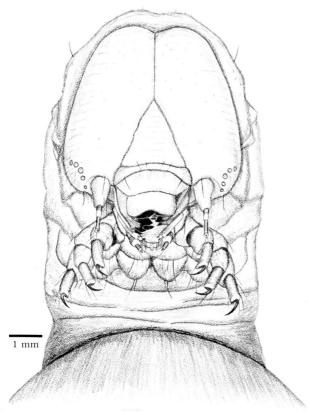

1 mm

3.42. FRONT VIEW OF A MOTH CATERPILLAR.

Leaf Chewers

MEETING AN INSECT face to face gives you a good view of the jaws it uses for chewing (Fig. 3.42). It is jaws like these that chew leaves and pulverize wood. The jaws of this **caterpillar,** as well as those of other insects, are made of extra-thick, dark cuticle. When a caterpillar has a good appetite, its jaws can make short order of the leaves you serve it.

The eyes of caterpillars are not those two large domes on each side of its face but are those ten small circles, five on each side of its jaws. Each one of these eyes is a simple eye or *ocellus* (little eye). Each ocellus is constructed like a single ommatidium in the large compound eye of a dragonfly (see Fig. 2.32). These ocelli cannot see all the details that a compound eye can see, but a caterpillar can scan its surroundings and piece together an overall picture of the scene around it.

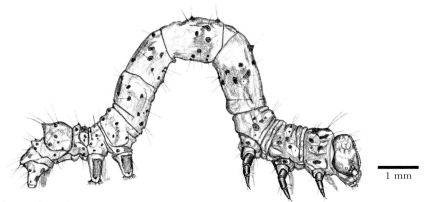

1 mm

Inchworms slink along by drawing their posterior ends up to their front legs (Fig. 3.43). In this way the back end keeps pace with the front end, and the body segments in between form a loop that straightens as the front end inches forward. While other caterpillars have five pairs of false legs on their abdomens, inchworms have only two or three pairs. Without the usual number of these false abdominal legs, inchworms have resorted to the unique style of locomotion that has earned them other equally descriptive names—measuring worms, spanworms, loopers, and geometers (*geo,* earth; *metron,* measure).

You can encounter inchworms in many places and in many forms. One of them might just plop down on your arm and begin pacing off the distance between your wrist and elbow. Some pose as twigs or sticks; others that are not as naturally camouflaged cover themselves with silk and pieces of leaves or flower petals. Some of us know inchworms as the caterpillars that dangle for a time on fine silk threads and then eventually scramble back up their silk ropes. On summer evenings most of us have also seen the slim moths that are the adult forms of the inchworms. It seems fitting that the wings of many geometer moths are covered with handsome, geometric patterns.

Although **bagworms** (Fig. 3.44) are really tree dwellers, the trees they like the best, cedars and junipers, happen to be common in many pastures and clearings.

Bagworms do things in very different ways. Living in a bag certainly seems strange, but other insects, such as caddis fly larvae, do this. What is different about bagworms is that the females never leave their bags—not even for courting, mating, or egg laying. They just lie waiting in their bags when the males fly around and come courting. After this one "fling," the wingless female lays her eggs and dies. Inside the bag, the eggs will weather winter storms protected by many layers of silk and the remains of their mother's body.

If you collect a few of these bags from an evergreen in late winter or early spring, you can perform an interesting experiment. Place the bags and some sprigs of the evergreen on which you found them in a covered jar or terrarium. In a few days, tiny bagworms will start sallying forth. One of the first things they will do is to begin making their bags. To the silk that they spin, they add pieces of leaves, twigs, or whatever else happens to be in the vicinity. If you pro-

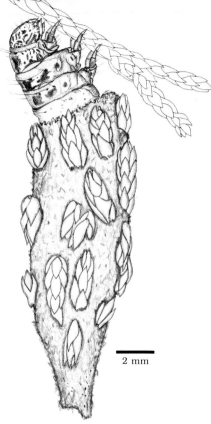

3.44. BAGWORM.

2 mm

vide the bagworms with small pieces of colored yarn, you will discover that they will fasten some of these to their bag. You might also learn about the bagworms' tastes in colors.

3.45. TORTOISE BEETLE.

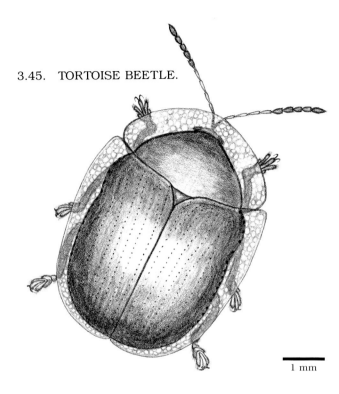

1 mm

Leaf beetles are a large family of small beetles. **Flea beetles, case-bearing beetles,** and **tortoise beetles** are only a few members of this big family. What they lack in size is often compensated for by their striking colors and patterns, often metallic hues that give their owners the appearance of tiny gems among the leaves and stems.

The golden tortoise beetle (Fig. 3.45) must have been the insect that inspired Edgar Allan Poe to write *The Gold Bug.* In the words of the story's main character, a fellow named Legrand, "It is the loveliest thing in creation." Now Legrand might have been a little overenthusiastic, but you too will probably be delighted to find such a treasure among the weeds or tangles of bindweed and morning glory, where these tortoise-shaped beetles usually dwell.

The iridescent gold of the tortoise beetle is imparted by the play of sunlight on thin films of liquid and cuticle within the exoskeleton.

Light travels as waves from the sun and comes as a mixture of colors—in fact, all the colors of the rainbow. Each color has its own wavelength, that is, the distance between two wave peaks.

Just as light is reflected at each surface of a soap bubble, so also is it reflected from every surface of the films of liquid and cuticle in the beetle's exoskeleton. All the colors of sunlight strike the surfaces, but only certain colors bounce back

101

to our eyes; these are the orange and yellow wavelengths that impart the rich gold iridescence to this handsome beetle. But what happens to red, green, and blue after they strike the exoskeleton? The wavelengths of these colors do not interact with films in the exoskeleton in quite the same way as the wavelengths of orange and yellow.

Figure 3.46 shows what happens when two light beams from the sun strike the surface of the tortoise beetle's exoskeleton. In both diagrams,

beam *1* is reflected from the lower surface of the film and beam *2* is reflected from the upper surface. When the two beams consist of short-wavelength light (green, blue), the reflected waves (*1 + 2*) are out of phase and cancel each other out, so we do not see these colors (Fig. 3.46A). However, when the two beams consist of long-wavelength light (orange, yellow), the reflected waves (*1 + 2*) are in phase and we see a gold color (Fig. 3.46B).

As the film thickness in cuticles changes, so

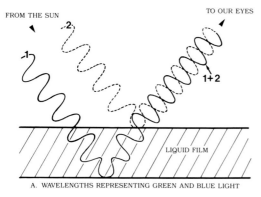

A. WAVELENGTHS REPRESENTING GREEN AND BLUE LIGHT

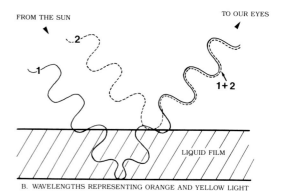

B. WAVELENGTHS REPRESENTING ORANGE AND YELLOW LIGHT

3.46.   WHY THE GOLDEN TORTOISE BEETLE IS GOLD.

do the colors whose wavelengths happen to be in phase and are reflected to our eyes. You will probably notice that the tortoise beetle is not always in a golden mood. When the beetle is annoyed or when it is dead, its cuticle loses water, the film thickness changes, and the tortoise beetle loses its luster.

The interplay of light within thin films in other exoskeletons is responsible for the colorful glitter of many insects and spiders that you will encounter.

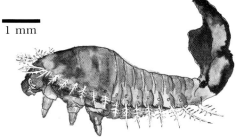

A. LARVA OF IRIDESCENT GOLDEN TORTOISE BEETLE

Tortoise beetle larvae are fascinating insect characters in their own right. On the same weeds where you find the golden adults, you are very likely to come across the spiny larvae, but you might not even notice them at first because of their outlandish attire. Each larva has a long fork at the end of its abdomen on which the outgrown skins are carried like a parasol over its back (Fig. 3.47). Some people think the wad of shed skins looks more like a backpack and call the larvae "peddlers." A little extra luggage probably makes travel over the morning glory vines safer.

B. LARVA OF NONIRIDESCENT TORTOISE BEETLE

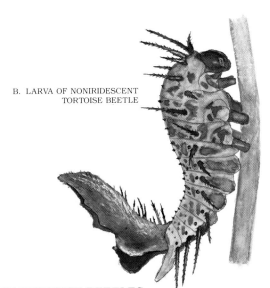

3.47. SPINY LARVAE OF TORTOISE BEETLES.

103

Flea beetles (Fig. 3.48) can be found throughout the meadow, and many are likely to end up in your net as you sweep it through the weeds. Flea beetles are probably best known for their destructive deeds in the garden. Most gardeners, at one time or another, have seen the leaves of their radishes and beans riddled by hordes of these hopping beetles.

Like their namesakes the fleas, these beetles have hind legs equipped with bulging jumping muscles. The powerful legs can propel the flea beetle a foot or more through the air—an impressive feat for such a tiny creature, especially when you consider that it is jumping over a hundred times its height.

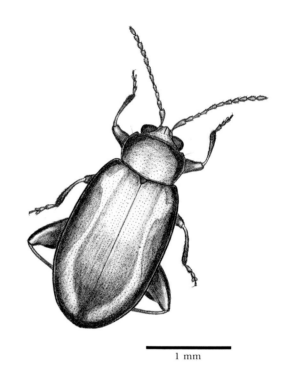

1 mm

3.48. FLEA BEETLE.

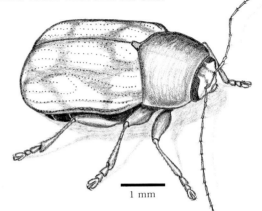

1 mm

Roaming the leaves of some meadow plants are dark specks that look just like caterpillar droppings. On closer inspection, however, they are the mobile homes of **case-bearing leaf beetle larvae** (Fig. 3.49). Like their relatives the tortoise beetles, these larvae do not discard their outgrown skins but use them in building their deceptive cases. Not only do they feed from these cases, but they also pupate in them.

The **case-bearing leaf beetles** that finally emerge come in a profusion of colors and patterns (Fig. 3.50); nature has been generous in designing handsome patterns of spots and stripes, which probably has its hazards. These beetles have lost their disguise as caterpillar droppings, thus must become escape artists by tucking in all six legs and their two long antennae and quickly dropping to safety. Once among the tangled undergrowth of weeds and grass, they can then amble back at their leisure to the leaves above.

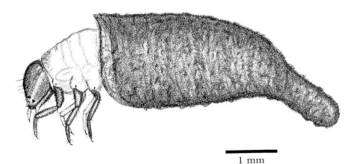

1 mm

3.49. CASE-BEARING LEAF BEETLE LARVA.

105

What is poison for one creature may be the main course for some other creature. Dining on milkweed is not recommended for people, but there are many insects that dine on nothing else. At least these insects do not have to worry about larger animals eating their milkweeds; horses and cows certainly avoid them and even foolhardy goats turn up their noses at them. Not only do larger grazers shun milkweeds, but birds and other large predators keep clear of milkweed insects because the insects transfer the poisonous chemicals from milkweed sap to their own blood. The would-be predators are warned by the bright red and orange warning colors of the insects.

Milkweed plants have a set of midsummer residents on their blossoms and another set of late summer and fall residents on their seed pods. Visitors such as flies, bees, and wasps stop by at both times of the year. We have already met the late summer residents that suck milkweed sap—orange milkweed bugs and yellow milkweed aphids (see Fig. 3.2)—so now let us meet some of the midsummer residents (Fig. 3.51).

3.51.   MIDSUMMER RESIDENTS OF MILKWEED.

106

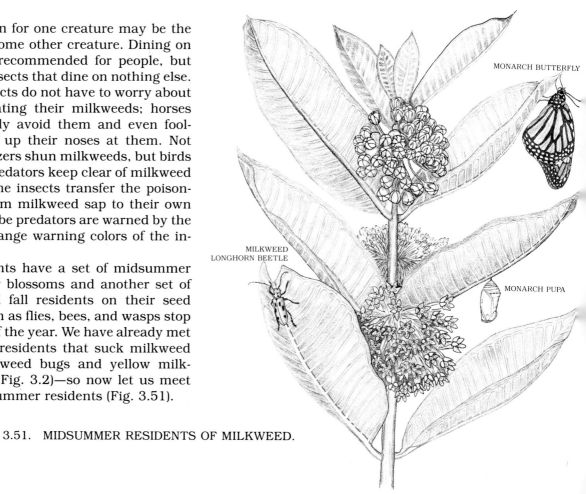

MONARCH BUTTERFLY

MILKWEED
LONGHORN BEETLE

MONARCH PUPA

At every stage of its life—from a yellow, white, and black **monarch caterpillar** (Fig. 3.52) to a black and orange butterfly—the monarch has a regal look about it. The chrysalis (*chrysos*, gold; *alis*, pertaining to) or pupa that hangs from the underside of a milkweed leaf looks as though it has been carved from jade and embroidered with spots and stripes of gold.

The monarch butterfly is one of the very few insects of northern latitudes that cannot survive cold and icy winters at any stage of its life cycle. Each fall monarchs undertake an awesome southward migration; each spring they migrate north as the milkweed starts growing again. The monarchs of the East winter on a small tract of land in the mountains of Mexico, where the butterflies gather by the millions. Can you imagine what a sight that must be? The government of Mexico has realized the value of this spot and has declared the area a sanctuary for the monarchs. Our West Coast monarchs that overwinter along the California coast are less fortunate. Their winter homes are still being destroyed by real estate developers. The United States, with all its wealth and influence, perhaps has a lesson to learn from the people of Mexico.

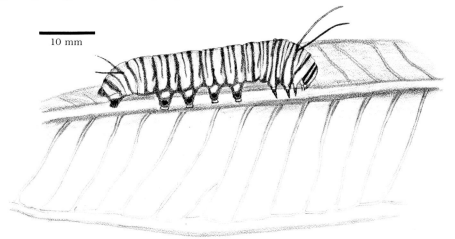

10 mm

3.52. MONARCH CATERPILLAR.

The **viceroy** is another butterfly that is also orange and black like the monarch, but it has an extra black bar that runs parallel to the outer edge of each of its hind wings. Adopting the looks of the unpalatable monarch has its payoffs. Most birds know to stay away from those orange and black warning colors, even though they are worn by an edible imposter.

Although the viceroy butterfly looks very much like a monarch butterfly, the tan and cream chrysalis of the viceroy (Fig. 3.53) bears little resemblance to the monarch chrysalis. The viceroy caterpillar also does not have much in common with the monarch caterpillar; as a caterpillar, the viceroy chews on willow or poplar leaves and is blotched rather than striped like the monarch caterpillar.

3.53.   CHRYSALIS OF THE VICEROY BUTTERFLY.

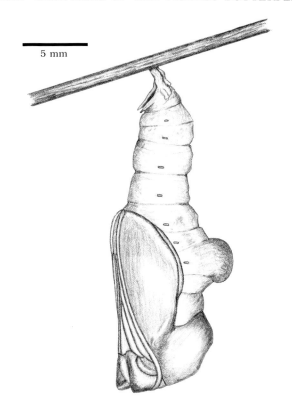

5 mm

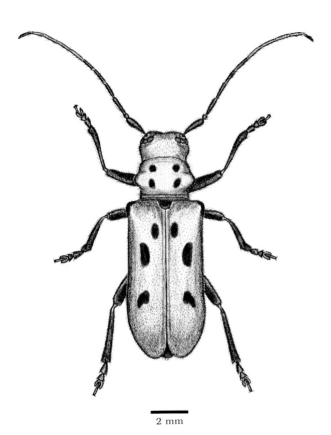

2 mm

3.54. MILKWEED LONGHORN BEETLE.

The monarch shares its summer domain with black and red **longhorn beetles** (Fig. 3.54). The adult beetles are summer residents of the leaves and flowers, and their round-headed larvae are residents in milkweed roots during the rest of the year. These beetles are easy to catch but protest at being held by making high-pitched squeaks. Hold one long enough to look into its eyes—all four of them. Two eyes above its antennae and two eyes below its antennae give it a broad view from the milkweed plant.

109

3.55. MILKWEED LEAF BEETLE.

2 mm

The milkweed longhorn beetles are not the only beetles responsible for holes in the milkweed leaves. Pudgy, orange and black **milkweed leaf beetles** as well as their larvae do their share of leaf chewing too. These beetles overwinter as adults among clumps of weeds and roots in the meadow (Fig. 3.55). One of their favorite places to spend the winter is among the soft, fuzzy leaves of the mullein—that common yellow-flowered weed of meadows and fields. It is easy to imagine those woolly leaves being cozy blankets. As soon as the beetles roll out of their winter quarters, they head for some leafy food.

The creatures of meadows and fields have other talents that we still have not discussed. Talents such as leaf mining and gall making are shared with insects and mites that live on trees; we will consider some of these other talents in Chapter 4.

CLASSIFICATION

Class Arachnida
 Spiders
  Order Araneida (*aranea*, spider)
   Family Salticidae (*salticus*, of jumping): **jumping spider**
   Family Thomisidae (*thomis*, thread): **crab spider**

Class Insecta
 Grasshoppers, Crickets, Cockroaches, Mantises, Walkingsticks
  Order Orthoptera (*orthos*, straight; *ptera*, wings)
   Family Acrididae (*acridos*, grasshopper): **short-horned grasshopper**
   Family Tettigoniidae (*tettigos*, grasshopper or cicada): **long-horned grasshopper**
   Family Gryllidae (*gryllus*, cricket): **cricket**
   Family Mantidae (*mantis*, prophet): **praying mantis**

 Aphids, Cicadas, Hoppers, Psyllids, Spittle Bugs
  Order Homoptera (*homos*, same; *ptera*, wings)
   Family Aphididae (*aphis*, plant louse): **aphid**
   Family Cercopidae (*cercos*, tail; *pion*, fat): **spittle bug**
   Family Membracidae (*membrax*, a kind of cicada): **treehopper** nymph and adult
   Family Cicadellidae (*cicadella*, little cicada): **leafhopper**
   Family Cicadidae (*cicada*, cicada): **cicada**

 True Bugs
  Order Hemiptera (*hemi*, half; *ptera*, wings)
   Family Corimelaenidae (*coris*, bug; *melanos*, black): **negro bug**
   Family Lygaeidae (*lygaios*, shadowy, gloomy): **milkweed bug**
   Family Pentatomidae (*pente*, five; *tomos*, parts): **stink bug**
   Family Coreidae (*coreos*,bug): **leaf-footed bug**
   Family Phymatidae (*phymation*, little tumor, wart): **ambush bug**

111

Dobson Flies, Lacewings, Ant Lions
  Order Neuroptera (*neuron*, nerve; *ptera*, wings)
    Family Chrysopidae (*chrysos*, gold, *ops*, eye): **golden-eyed lacewing** larva and adult

True Flies
  Order Diptera (*dis*, two; *ptera*, wings)
    Family Dolichopodidae (*dolichos*, long; *poda*, feet): **long-legged fly**
    Family Syrphidae (*syrphos*, a kind of fly): **hover fly**
    Family Tachinidae (*tachinos*, swift): **tachinid fly**

Beetles
  Order Coleoptera (*coleos*, sheath; *ptera*, wings)
    Family Lampyridae (*lampyris*, glow worm): **firefly**
    Family Cantharidae (*cantharos*, a kind of beetle): **soldier beetle**
    Family Coccinellidae (*coccineus*, red; *-ellus*, little): **ladybird beetle** larva and adult
    Family Cerambycidae (*cerambyx*, a horned beetle): **milkweed longhorn beetle**
    Family Chrysomelidae (*chrysos*, gold; *meleos*, useless): **tortoise beetle** adult and larva; **flea beetle**;
      case-bearing leaf beetle adult and larva; **milkweed leaf beetle**

Butterflies, Moths
  Order Lepidoptera (*lepidos*, scale; *ptera*, wings)
    Family Nymphalidae (*nymphalis*, nymphlike): **painted lady** butterfly, **viceroy** pupa
    Family Geometridae (*geo*, earth; *metron*, measure): **inchworm, geometer**
    Family Psychidae (*psyche*, butterfly, moth): **bagworm**
    Family Danaidae (*da*, very; *naias*, nymphlike): **monarch** butterfly, pupa, and caterpillar

Ants, Bees, Wasps
  Order Hymenoptera (*hymen*, membrane; *ptera*, wings)
    Family Apidae (*apis*, bee): **honey bee**
    Family Formicidae (*formica*, ant): **ant**

4. Trees and Logs

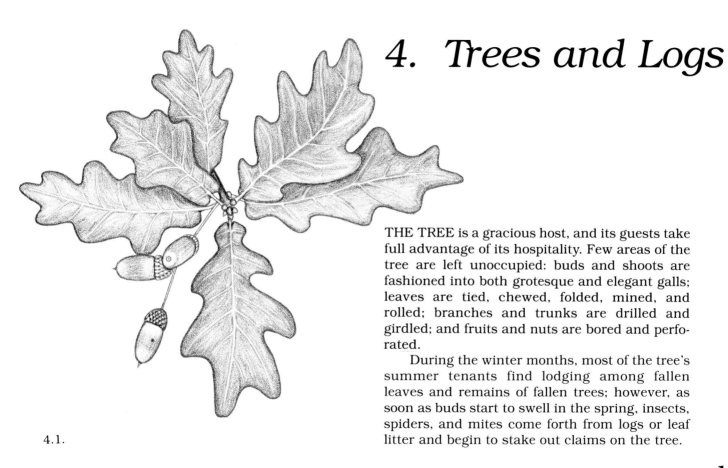

4.1.

THE TREE is a gracious host, and its guests take full advantage of its hospitality. Few areas of the tree are left unoccupied: buds and shoots are fashioned into both grotesque and elegant galls; leaves are tied, chewed, folded, mined, and rolled; branches and trunks are drilled and girdled; and fruits and nuts are bored and perforated.

During the winter months, most of the tree's summer tenants find lodging among fallen leaves and remains of fallen trees; however, as soon as buds start to swell in the spring, insects, spiders, and mites come forth from logs or leaf litter and begin to stake out claims on the tree.

113

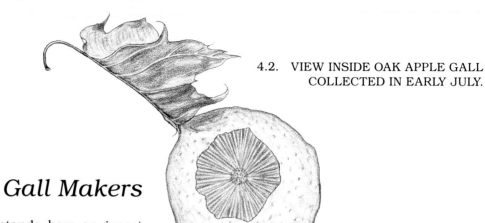

Gall Makers

NO ONE REALLY understands how an insect produces a gall (Fig. 4.2). Through a cooperative interaction, the insect and the plant somehow produce forms that the plant would never produce on its own. There is evidence that chemicals deposited during egg laying or contained in larval saliva stimulate growth of the plant gall, but how this growth generates a specific form and shape is still a mystery.

Many of the hundreds of different galls produced by insects and mites have marvelous forms. On a single oak tree, for example, a dozen different galls and gall makers can be found. The workmanship of each gall maker is unique, although each one may start with the same raw materials.

Tiny **gall wasps** (Fig. 4.3) are found primarily on oak trees. In fact, no fewer than a thousand different species of these wasps produce galls on oak trees, each gall having its own unique design.

In 1873 a German biologist demonstrated that many species of gall wasps come in two quite different forms and produce two quite different galls; so different is the appearance of the two forms of some wasp species and their galls that biologists had classified them as two different species. One form appears in early spring,

114

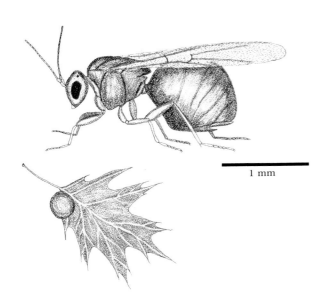

4.3. LEAF GALL AND FEMALE GALL WASP
THAT EMERGES IN EARLY SUMMER.

the other form appears in late spring or early
summer. In other words, gall wasps have al-
ternating generations.

As leaves and catkin flowers unfurl in early
spring (Fig. 4.4), gall wasps set about laying eggs
in tender oak shoots.

4.4. NEW LEAVES AND CATKINS ON AN OAK SHOOT.

115

There is something very unique about the first gall wasps that emerge in early spring from galls of the preceding year: they are all females. These females must manage their affairs alone for there are no males to court them or to fertilize their eggs. Although each of these female wasps had two parents, her sons and daughters hatch from unfertilized eggs and inherit only her genetic material; she is their only parent. The daughters and sons stay in their galls through the spring and then emerge and mate in early summer. The new generation of gall wasps that hatches from their fertilized eggs is again all female, and they follow in the footsteps of their grandmothers. They live in galls shaped like those of their grandmothers, not like those of their parents. The larvae feed during the summer, overwinter in their galls, and at last emerge as females in the nippy spring air, just as their grandmothers did the year before. Thus, the cycle continues from year to year—mothers, daughters and sons, granddaughters, etc. It all makes for a very strange family tree.

On some hackberry trees, almost every leaf has at least one nipple gall (Fig. 4.5A), which is made by a relative of aphids and cicadas—an insect known as a **psyllid** (pronounced sillid; *psylla,* flea). Throughout the summer, psyllid nymphs (Fig. 4.5B), which live inside the galls, sip hackberry juice with their beaks. By late summer the nymphs have matured and are ready to try their wings. On some September days, adult psyllids (Fig. 4.5C) fly by the thousands from hackberry trees in search of quiet spots in which to spend the winter months.

4.5. PSYLLID DEVELOPMENT.

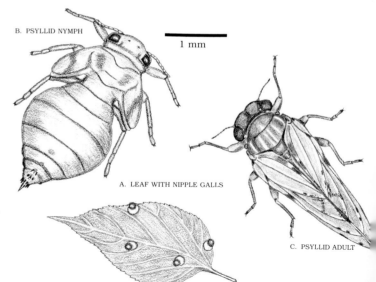

B. PSYLLID NYMPH

1 mm

A. LEAF WITH NIPPLE GALLS

C. PSYLLID ADULT

A project for September: wrap the ends of a few gall-covered leaves in a wet paper towel; be sure that you keep the towel wet so the leaves do not dry out. Place the leaves inside a covered jar. After a few days, adult psyllids should appear on the sides of the jar. They are very small, so look closely.

The apple gall is a common sight among patches of goldenrod in meadows and along roadsides (Fig. 4.6A). Nestled in the very center of the gall is a rotund, white grub that grows throughout the summer and rests throughout the winter (Fig. 4.6B). Before settling in for the cold months, the larva builds up reserves of several chemicals in its blood that act as an "antifreeze," which helps the larva survive subfreezing temperatures. Also, before the gall becomes hard and dry, the larva carves a tunnel to the surface of the gall. There it leaves only a thin plug to push aside when it finally makes its debut as a fly. The larva transforms into a pupa at the end of winter, and a **gall fly** with handsomely splotched wings (Fig. 4.6C) emerges in late April or early May.

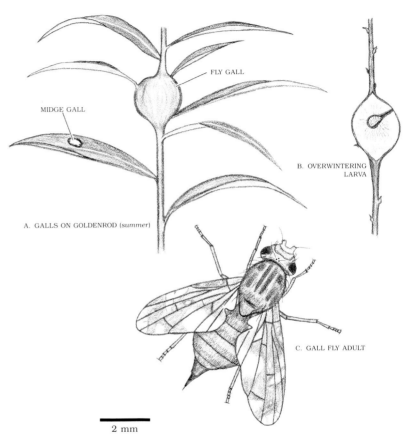

FLY GALL

MIDGE GALL

B. OVERWINTERING LARVA

A. GALLS ON GOLDENROD (*summer*)

C. GALL FLY ADULT

2 mm

4.6.   GALL FLY DEVELOPMENT.

117

Midges of the family Cecidomyiidae are often found in the company of fungi—on logs, under bark, or under fallen leaves. The larvae of this particular cecidomyiid midge, however, live in fungal galls on goldenrod leaves. Open one of the white blotches on a goldenrod leaf (Fig. 4.6A) and inside you will find a tiny larva of the **gall midge** (Fig. 4.7). The gall midge has developed a special partnership with a special fungus. At the spot where the female midge lays an egg on a goldenrod leaf, she also deposits some fungus. As the fungus grows, it not only provides food for the midge larva, but it probably also nurtures the growth of the gall.

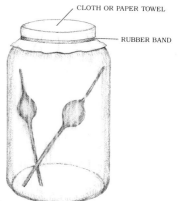

CLOTH OR PAPER TOWEL

RUBBER BAND

4.7. GALL MIDGE.

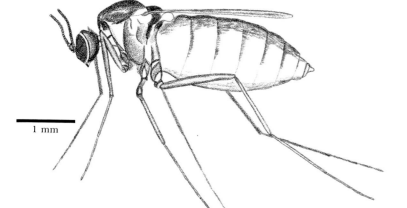

1 mm

4.8. JAR TERRARIUM.

Galls can be gathered from trees, shrubs, and weeds at almost any time of year. Those that are harvested in the fall and winter can be placed in a covered terrarium or jar (Fig. 4.8) located on a cool window ledge. If the plant tissue is still green, it should be kept moist until a creature appears from the gall chamber.

4.9. TORYMID WASP.

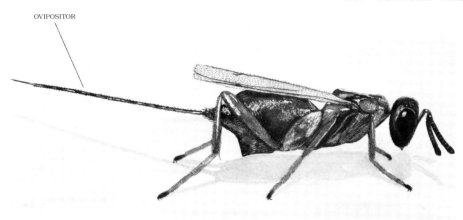

OVIPOSITOR

1 mm

What emerges from a gall may not always be the maker of the gall. Certain small wasps, such as the **torymid wasp** (Fig. 4.9), specialize in locating galls as nurseries for their parasitic larvae. The female wasp uses her long ovipositor to probe a gall until she finds the chamber occupied by the larva of the gall maker and then deposits her eggs. So do not be surprised if more than one species of insect emerges from the galls that you collect, even though the galls all look alike.

ALTHOUGH from our perspective leaves are very flat and thin, most of them are thick enough to house a number of larval insects between their upper and lower surfaces. These tiny larvae, however, must be specially adapted to live in these tight quarters. The body of a **leaf miner** is usually flat, the legs are quite short or even absent, and the jaws move like pruning shears within the plane of the leaf. Only a few groups of insects have taken up this life style, and they are all found among the beetles, true flies, sawflies, and moths.

Miners vary in their approaches to leaf excavation. Some construct full-depth mines between the upper and lower epidermis of the leaf, others mine only the upper palisade layer (Fig. 4.10), while some mine only the lower spongy layer.

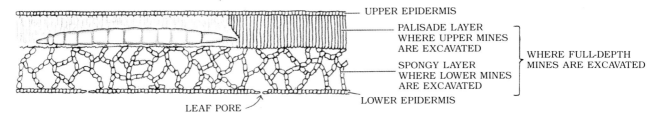

UPPER EPIDERMIS

PALISADE LAYER
WHERE UPPER MINES
ARE EXCAVATED

SPONGY LAYER
WHERE LOWER MINES
ARE EXCAVATED

LOWER EPIDERMIS

WHERE FULL-DEPTH
MINES ARE EXCAVATED

LEAF PORE

4.10.   LEAF MINER LARVA IN UPPER PALISADE LAYER OF A LEAF.

The leaves of black locust trees are popular homes for some **leaf miner larvae.** The larva in Figure 4.11 digs a full-depth mine in a leaflet.

Leaf miners can be easily reared at home if you pick the short branch on which the mine is located and keep it in a jar of water in your terrarium. Hold the leaf mine toward the sky whenever you inspect it. Because it is so thin, daylight readily penetrates the leaf and silhouettes the slightly denser leaf miner. Watch how the mine expands as the larva continues excavating, and notice how the miner disposes of its droppings and shed skins. Some miners are extremely fastidious and excavate a special chamber for their garbage.

It should be no surprise that, although the leaf provides a safe haven from sun, rain, and birds, there are parasitic wasps that still manage to probe leaf mines with their ovipositors. The mine that you inspect might harbor one of these parasites, but often the leaf miner itself will appear.

4.11. LEAF MINER LARVA FROM A BLACK LOCUST LEAF MINE (*arrow*).

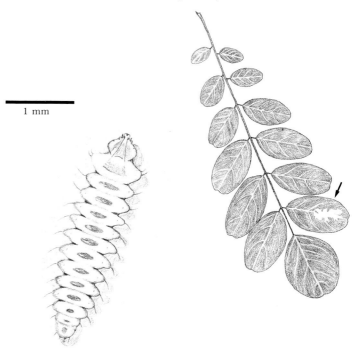

1 mm

Colorful black and orange **leaf-mining bee-tles** emerge from the mines on black locust leaves (Fig. 4.12). They rarely wander far from their larval home but stay to feed on the outside of the leaves.

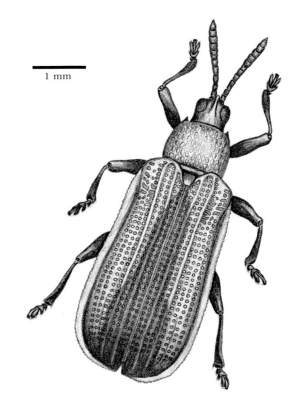

1 mm

4.12.   LOCUST LEAF-MINING BEETLE.

1 mm

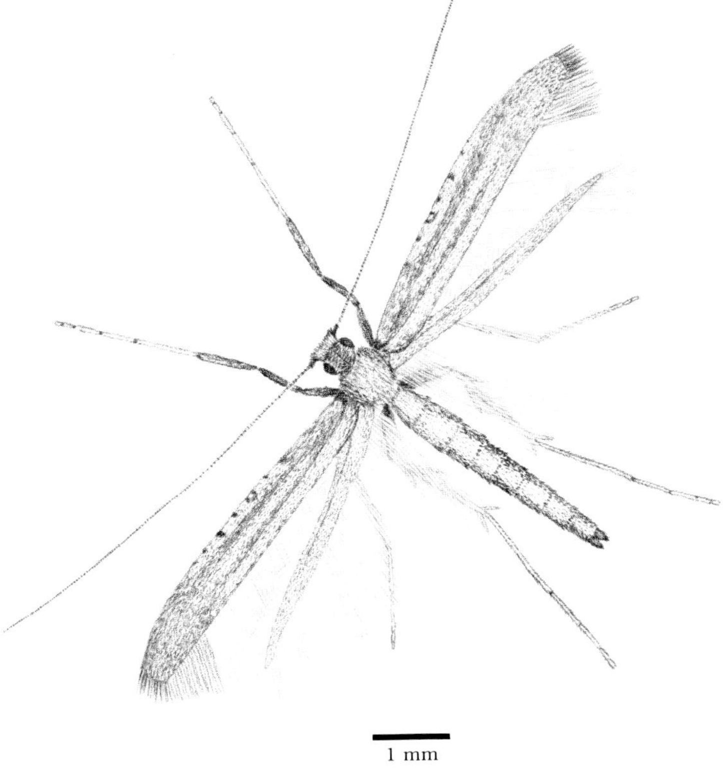

A group of tiny brown and white **leaf-mining moths** has distinguished itself as the largest family of leaf-mining insects in the world (Fig. 4.13). The botanical tastes of this group are all-embracing, but each species of moth has its own preference for a particular species of plant. Not even poison ivy is too mean to be the palace for some of these moth larvae. The itchy oil of poison ivy is localized in the upper and lower epidermal layers of each leaf (see Fig. 4.10), and sandwiched between these two layers lies the tissue that the larva excavates and devours in late summer.

123

Drillers, Borers, and Engravers

ON A TRIP to the woods, take some time to look on and under the bark of a rotting log. Although a fallen tree no longer sustains a canopy of leaves or a network of roots and is considered dead, it still sustains many lives within its lifeless form. You are very likely to encounter many of the creatures of leaf litter and soil, such as cen- tipedes and springtails, but there will probably be some new acquaintances as well.

A thick mat of mosses, liverworts, and lichens may blanket the log, and a mushroom or two may have sprouted in their midst (Fig. 4.14). In this miniature forest the mosses tower like trees over many creatures, and the mushrooms loom like skyscrapers.

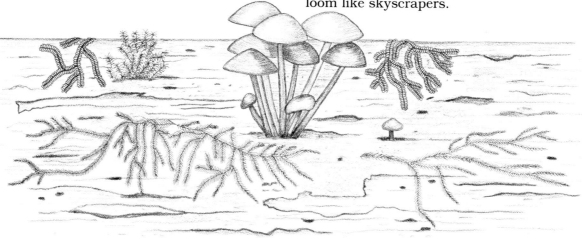

4.14. FALLEN LOG WITH MOSSES, LIVERWORTS, AND FUNGI.

Peering into this forest, you may come upon an otherworldly insect with a large belly and big eyes that will probably be scuttling about, nibbling on mosses or chewing on fungi. This tiny animal happens to be a **bark louse** (Fig. 4.15), the country relative of the pale and wingless **book louse** (Fig. 4.16).

The book louse seems to prefer town living to country living and is a fancier of peeling wallpaper and old books. You might even find a book louse munching on the pages of this book after a few years. Fortunately, they eat very little. Book lice have found that the taste of books, like that of certain cheeses, improves with age.

4.16. BOOK LOUSE.

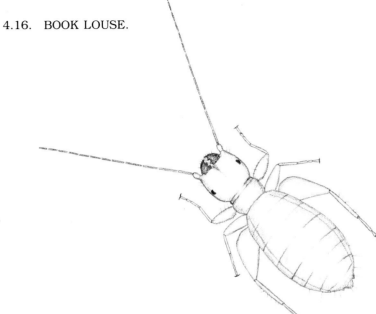

0.5 mm

4.15. BARK LOUSE.

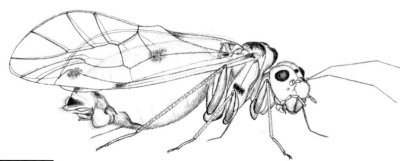

1 mm

125

If the log you are examining is an oak log, there may be some other comical-looking creatures about, the weevils. What makes these insects stand out is their snouts. You do not expect to find jaws on the ends of these long snouts but that is what you do find; the beetles use them as drills. The beetles with the long snouts are **acorn weevils;** the ones with the shorter snouts are **wood-boring weevils** (Fig. 4.17). Into each of the holes they drill in a log or acorn, female weevils drop one of their eggs.

As long as a squirrel or parasitic wasp does

2 mm

4.17. WOOD-BORING WEEVIL.

not discover its acorn, the grub (larva) of the acorn weevil grows until autumn. When its acorn falls from the oak tree, the grub ventures forth to burrow into the ground, where it will pass the winter awaiting the return of warm weather to pupate and eventually grow a snout of its own (Figs. 4.18 and 4.19).

Look around for acorns that have been drilled. If it is not too late in the fall, they probably will still contain weevil grubs. Put the drilled acorns in a jar with soil and leaves. Leave them outside during the winter and some day the following year, a long-nosed weevil may be looking out at you.

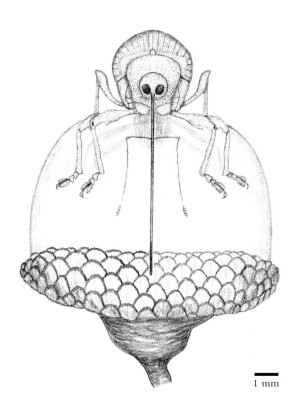

2 mm

1 mm

4.19. ACORN WEEVIL ON ACORN (*front view*).

127

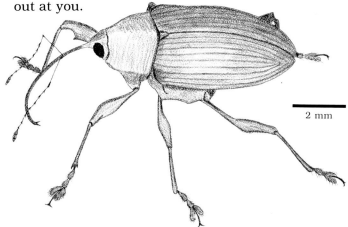

4.18. ACORN WEEVIL (*side view*).

Many beetles and their larvae live in the narrow world between the bark and the heartwood of the log—the thin, tender layer called the cambium. It is a tight squeeze, and to live there an insect either has to be small or flat or both small and flat.

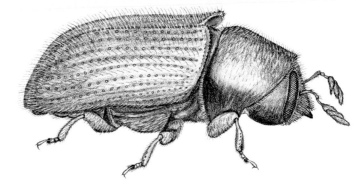

4.20. ENGRAVER BEETLE.

1 mm

Tiny **engraver beetles** (Fig. 4.20) etch their galleries beneath the bark, each species having its own distinctive signature. The etched pattern is actually a family effort. The mother beetle begins the etching by tunneling through the bark to construct the central brood gallery along the sides of which she lays her eggs. Each newly hatched larva then sets off on a course more or less at right angles to the brood gallery (Fig. 4.21); each larva is able to steer between the tightly spaced, parallel tunnels being built on either side by its brothers and sisters. As the larvae grow, the tunnels lengthen and widen until each larva undergoes metamorphosis at the end of its tunnel. From these ornate etchings in the cambium of the log, you can learn a great deal about the family history of engraver beetles.

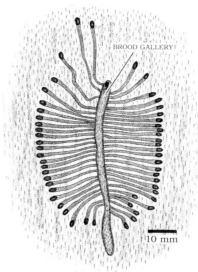

BROOD GALLERY

10 mm

4.21. GALLERIES OF ENGRAVER BEETLES.

4.22. HAMMERHEAD BORER.

Some odd-shaped larvae with hammerheads live within wider, less ornate tunnels in the cambium. They are considerably larger than engraver beetles—at least in length and width; but they are flattened in the third dimension. The bulging head and thorax of a **hammerhead borer** (Fig. 4.22) hold the large muscles that power its wood-chewing jaws.

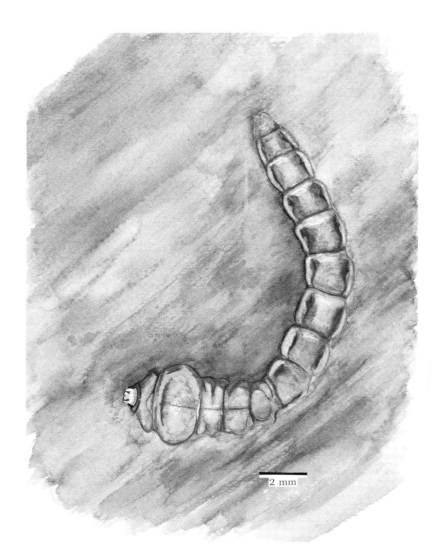

2 mm

Insect metamorphosis is filled with surprises. Who would ever guess that hammerhead borers would grow into metallic or bronzed beetles that can sometimes be found around logs but often visit flowers for a sip of nectar? These beetles are called **metallic wood borers** (Fig. 4.23), but the larvae are really the borers.

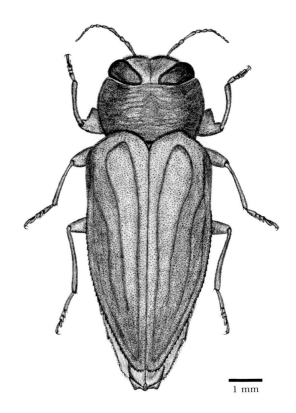

1 mm

4.23. METALLIC WOOD BORER.

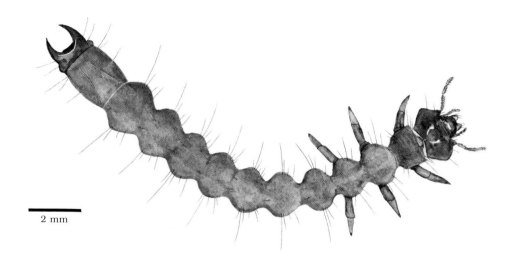

Other larvae that will catch your eye, if they are around, are the **fire-colored beetle larvae** (Fig. 4.24). These very flat larvae with formidable-looking, but harmless, tail pincers can be very common under the bark of some logs. The parent beetles, with their long, feathery antennae and their fire-colored markings, are more common at porch lights on summer evenings.

4.24.   FIRE-COLORED BEETLE LARVA.

131

Some carnivorous beetles never leave the logs of their youth, so we should not be surprised to discover that, even after metamorphosis, they maintain their flat shapes. What is surprising is that in this dark and hidden world there are such beautiful colors as the bright scarlet of **flat bark beetles** (Fig. 4.25) and the obsidian black of **hister beetles** (Fig. 4.26).

4.26. HISTER BEETLE.

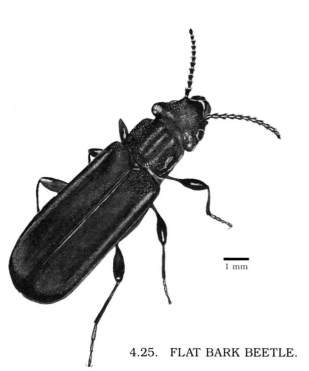

1 mm

132

4.25. FLAT BARK BEETLE.

Another surprise is that wood-boring insects are unable to digest most wood without some assistance. They do find small amounts of digestible sap and starch among the tough wood fibers, but if it were not for the many fungi that break down the fibers, the pickings would be very slim. The filaments of fungi wind and twist throughout the log, breaking down the wood fibers into substances that the insects can use. The filaments of fungi open the frontier of the solid heartwood beyond the bark and cambium. Once fungi gain a foothold in the heartwood, another group of borers follows in their trail. Some of them, like the **carpenter ants** (Fig. 4.27) and **termites** (Fig. 4.28), carry their own wood-digesting fungi, bacteria, or one-celled animals called protozoa (*protos,* first; *zoon,* animal).

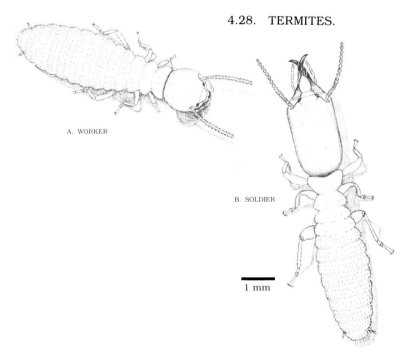

4.28.   TERMITES.

A. WORKER

B. SOLDIER

1 mm

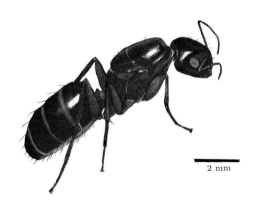

2 mm

4.27.   CARPENTER ANT.

Wireworms and roundhead borers are some of the first larvae to invade the heartwood of a log. With their sturdy jaws, they shape their galleries to their rounded bodies. When their days of woodcarving come to an end, the soft, white roundhead grubs pupate and develop into broad-shouldered **longhorn beetles** with long antennae (Fig. 4.29).

4.29. LONGHORN BEETLE.

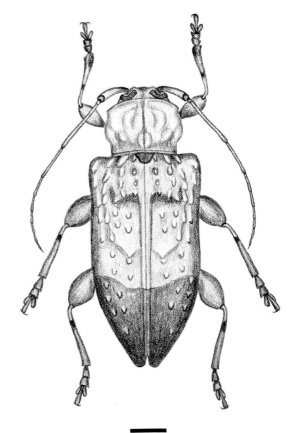

1 mm

Click beetles (Fig. 4.30) are the parents of the long, stiff wireworms. You might find these beetles around logs, but you are just as likely to see them on flowers or around evening lights.

Click beetles happen to be among the most acrobatic of insects, and their stunt is one that cannot be duplicated by any other insect. Like some other insects, these beetles fold their legs close to their bodies when disturbed and fall to the ground where they play possum until danger is past. Sometimes in falling to the ground, the beetle lands on its back and is unable to right

134

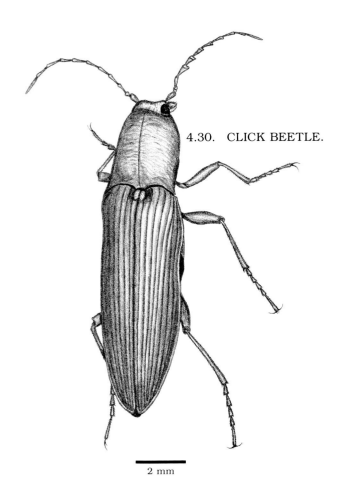

4.30. CLICK BEETLE.

2 mm

itself with its feet. When finding itself in this situation, the beetle resorts to its clicking stunt. At a loose joint on its thorax, the click beetle begins bending from the muscle tension that develops until it is cocked like a gun (Fig. 4.31). Then click! As the taut muscles suddenly relax, the beetle's back hits the ground with such force that it bounces several inches into the air. It may take more than one try, but the click beetle is a persistent creature and will eventually end up on its feet again.

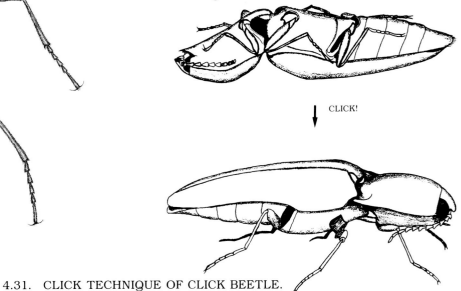

CLICK!

4.31. CLICK TECHNIQUE OF CLICK BEETLE.

135

2 mm

4.32. MELANDRYID BEETLE LARVA.

Other insects can gain access to the dark galleries of wireworms and roundheads. Predaceous beetle larvae, such as the larvae of the **melandryid beetle** (Fig. 4.32), roam the galleries and eat eggs, larvae, or pupae of the heartwood borers. Their sharp tail hooks give these predators good traction on their travels through the tunnels.

136

Female **ichneumon wasps** (Fig. 4.33) tap the surface of the log with their antennae and then probe the wood with their ovipositors. Their searching techniques seem baffling, but their ovipositors almost always find their marks. Ichneumons deposit their eggs in the tunnels of wood borers, where their parasitic larvae can easily find hosts to carry them through their larval days.

4.33.   FEMALE ICHNEUMON WASP.

5 mm

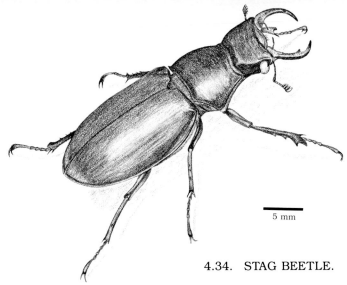

5 mm

4.34. STAG BEETLE.

small colonies. Adult beetles actually have been observed chewing wood and then feeding the tenderized morsels to their larvae. We expect this of bees, wasps, and ants, but not of other insects. What is also curious about these social beetles is that both larvae and adults squeak; scientists think they may be communicating with each other, but no one has yet deciphered their language. Pick one up and listen.

4.35. BESS BEETLE.

5 mm

After a log has been well-riddled with tunnels and strands of fungi, **stag beetles** (Fig. 4.34) and **bess beetles** (Fig. 4.35) begin to move in. These are some of our largest, but slowest, beetles. Bess beetles (family Passalidae: *passalos*, peg) sometimes go by the name of peg beetles; each beetle has a horn between its eyes that is shaped like a peg. These beetles are quite docile, but watch out for the jaws of the stag beetle.

If you find one bess beetle, you are likely to find several other adults and larvae. What is unusual about these beetles is that they live in

138

If you bring a plastic bag to the woods, you can return with a few pieces of rotten wood, some bark that is covered with vegetation (Fig. 4.36), and maybe a mushroom or two. After you have looked in on the lives of the log dwellers, however, remember to replace the remaining bark and hunks of log that you removed. All homes and habitats, including the log, should be respected.

After you arrive home, place the pieces of log in a large jar and then cover the mouth of the jar with a piece of cloth and a rubber band. What you did not see on or in the log on your trip to the woods may appear several days or several weeks later in your jar. Be ready for some surprises.

A. MOSS

B. LIVERWORT

1 mm

4.36.   VEGETATION APT TO BE FOUND ON BARK.

139

CLASSIFICATION

Class Insecta
    Termites
        Order Isoptera (*isos*, equal; *ptera*, wings)
            Family Rhinotermitidae (*rhinos*, beak; *termes*, insect that eats wood): **termite**

    Aphids, Cicadas, Hoppers, Psyllids, Spittle Bugs
        Order Homoptera (*homos*, same; *ptera*, wings)
            Family Psyllidae (*psylla*, flea): **psyllid** nymph and adult

    Bark Lice, Book Lice
        Order Psocoptera (*psocos*, chewer; *ptera*, wings)
            Family Pseudocaeciliidae (*pseudes*, false; *caecilia*, a kind of lizard): **bark louse**
            Family Liposcelidae (*lipos*, fat; *scelos*, leg): **book louse**

    True Flies
        Order Diptera (*dis*, two; *ptera*, wings)
            Family Cecidomyiidae (*cecidos*, gall; *myia*, fly): **gall midge**
            Family Tephritidae (*tephritis*, an ash-colored stone): **goldenrod gall fly**

    Beetles
        Order Coleoptera (*coleos*, sheath; *ptera*, wings)
            Family Histeridae (*hister*, actor): **hister beetle**
            Family Elateridae (*elater*, a driver): **click beetle**
            Family Buprestidae (*buprestis*, a kind of beetle): **metallic wood borer, hammerhead borer**
            Family Cucujidae (*cucuj* [Brazilian], a kind of beetle): **flat bark beetle**
            Family Pyrochroidae (*pyros*, fire; *chroia*, color): **fire-colored beetle** larva
            Family Melandryidae (*melanos*, dark; *dryas*, wood nymph): **melandryid beetle** larva
            Family Passalidae (*passalos*, peg): **bess beetle**

Family Lucanidae (*lucanus*, a kind of beetle): **stag beetle**
Family Cerambycidae (*cerambyx*, a horned beetle): **longhorn beetle**
Family Chrysomelidae (*chrysos*, gold; *meleos*, useless): **locust leaf miner** adult and larva
Family Brentidae (*brenthos*, haughtiness): **wood-boring weevil**
Family Curculionidae (*curculio*, weevil): **acorn weevil**
Family Scolytidae (*scolyt*, shorten): **engraver beetle**

Butterflies, Moths
    Order Lepidoptera (*lepidos*, scale; *ptera*, wings)
        Family Gracilariidae (*gracilis*, slender; *area*, space): **leaf-mining moth**

Ants, Bees, Wasps
    Order Hymenoptera (*hymen*, membrane; *ptera*, wings)
        Family Cynipidae (*cynips*, a gall insect): **gall wasp**
        Family Ichneumonidae (*ichneumon*, a tracker): **ichneumon wasp**
        Family Torymidae (*toros*, borer): parasitic **torymid wasp**
        Family Formicidae (*formica*, ant): **carpenter ant**

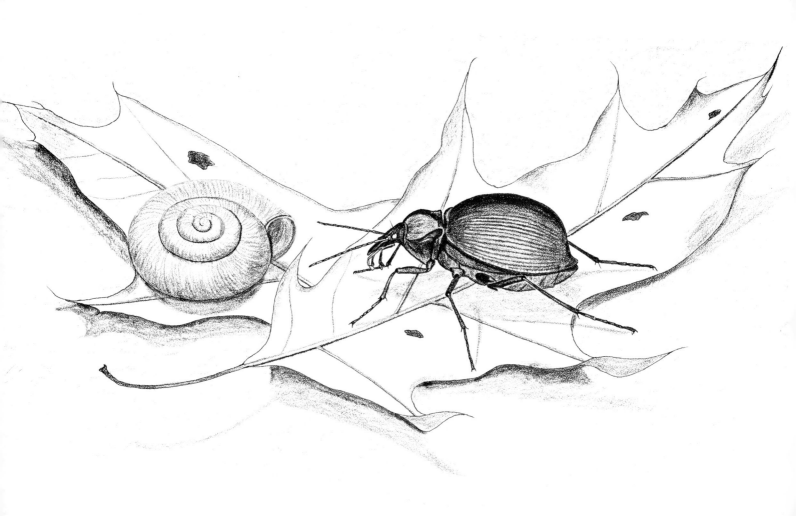

5.1

5. Beneath Our Feet

Every part of nature teaches that the passing away of one life is the making room for another.

—HENRY DAVID THOREAU

RECYCLING employs a large crew of arthropods, but the arthropods cannot manage alone. Other organisms—mosses, liverworts, earthworms, fungi, bacteria, snails—also have important jobs in returning the remains of plants and animals to the soil. The recycling business really requires a great deal of teamwork.

At the meeting of earth and sky, the efforts of the recyclers decide the fates of future generations of plants and animals. Ultimately, the survival of every plant and animal depends on the nutrients that are salvaged from the remains of past generations. The recyclers obviously have a great responsibility in nature's economy. Only by virtue of their astronomic numbers can these tiny creatures accomplish the staggering job of clearing the earth of tons of fallen leaves, logs, and animal remains.

By converting plant and animal matter to soil, the recyclers also create habitat for other animals—both year-round and winter residents. With the approach of cold weather, recycling practically comes to a halt; many permanent residents of the soil descend to levels that are insulated from the harsh winter temperatures aboveground. Refugees from the overlying canopies of trees and grasses drift into the leaf litter and soil to overwinter or to cache their eggs before the first heavy frosts quickly bring a halt to their activities or even their lives.

A winter census of the top layers of the soil would reveal an amazing diversity of transient species. In the fall many moth larvae descend into the soil from surrounding vegetation to pupate. Clutches of fly, beetle, and grasshopper eggs lie dormant among the bulbs and seeds that will be the vegetation next year. Some of the more delicately constructed adult insects will endure the rigors of winter on the forest floor. Along with the sturdier bumble bee queens and full-grown stink bugs, lacewings, ladybird beetles, and leafhoppers await the coming of spring in the soil and leaf litter.

Eventually, frost and snow cover hushed pastures and forest undergrowth. The life that abounded on the grass and trees is silenced for the winter season, but the promise of life holds forth among the plant remains and beneath the sod.

The first creatures that we will discuss in this chapter are not insects or, for that matter, spiders, but all of them are close relatives of insects and spiders. Like most of their soil-dwelling relatives, these creatures adapt very readily to life in a terrarium.

Mites have the distinction of being the most abundant eight-legged creatures on our planet, and certainly among the most widely distributed. Trees, ponds, meadows, soil—all the common habitats we consider in this book—are dwelling places for mites. Even uncommon habitats like butterfly ears and beetle bellies are home to some mites.

You can get some inkling of their abundance in the leaf litter in the woods or your backyard by setting up a very simple collecting device called a Berlese funnel, named after an Italian entomologist who first used one (Fig. 5.2).

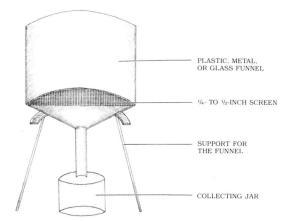

PLASTIC, METAL, OR GLASS FUNNEL

¼- TO ½-INCH SCREEN

SUPPORT FOR THE FUNNEL

COLLECTING JAR

5.2. CUT-AWAY VIEW OF A BERLESE FUNNEL.

As the leaf litter that you place on the screen in the funnel begins to dry, mites and other small creatures that you scooped up with the leaves will fall through the screen, down the funnel spout, and into the collecting jar. How many different mites do you find? A large (by mite standards), common mite is the scarlet **red velvet mite** that feeds on the eggs of other small animals in the leaf litter (Fig. 5.3).

1 mm   5.4. SPRINGTAIL.

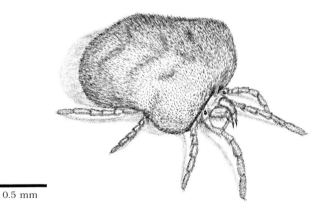

0.5 mm

5.3. RED VELVET MITE.

You might also notice some other six-legged creatures jumping about in the bottom of the jar. These may be **springtails** (Fig. 5.4). They do not have the powerful leg muscles like grasshoppers and flea beetles, but they do have strong muscles in their tails. Springtails carry their tails under their abdomens and catapult themselves by flicking their tails down and back.

Springtails are in a unique group of their own. They are not considered true insects, since their abdomens have fewer segments than the abdomens of insects. They also cannot be grouped with spiders, centipedes, or mites; they only have 6 legs. They have body parts that no other creatures have: of course, there is the

145

spring-loaded tail, and then there is a ventral peg behind its legs on the first segment of the abdomen. Although no one is really certain what this ventral peg does, it probably helps the springtail tighten its grip to the moist surfaces over which it crawls. The peg can only be seen from below as the springtail crawls over a clear surface, so if you look closely at the side of the collecting jar, you might notice it sticking to the glass. It is from this unique peg that springtails received the official scientific name for their order Collembola (*colla,* glue; *embolos,* peg).

Sow bugs and **pill bugs** are crustaceans like lobsters and shrimp, but they inhabit the land rather than the sea. Collectively, sow bugs and pill bugs are referred to as wood lice. They both look like little tanks lumbering over the rough terrain of the soil, but the pill bug is a more limber acrobat than the sow bug. Sow bugs (Fig. 5.5) simply cannot touch their heads to their tails, but if you gently tap a pill bug with your finger, it will quickly roll into a ball (Fig. 5.6) and wait until the intruding finger disappears. The scientific name for the genus of the pill bug, *Armadillidium,* is a reminder of the fact that armadillos employ the same escape tactic.

Mother wood lice carry their eggs and newly hatched young in pouches on the lower surface of their bodies—so kangaroos and koala bears are not the only animals to carry their young in brood pouches. When you look into your terrarium or under a board in the yard, watch for a mother wood louse that moves rather slowly and looks rather chubby. She probably has a pouch full of young that will shortly descend her legs and set out on their own.

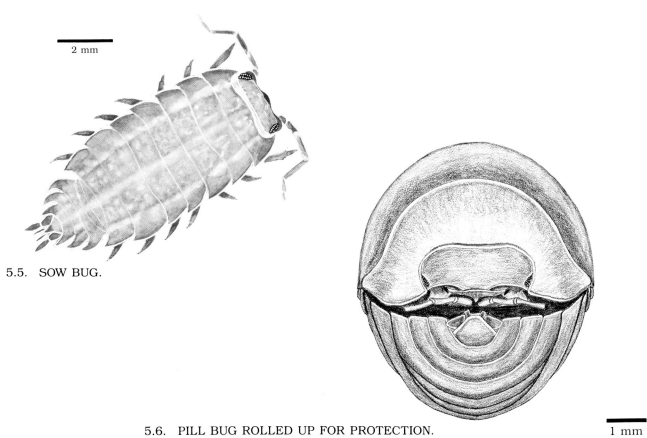

2 mm

5.5. SOW BUG.

1 mm

5.6. PILL BUG ROLLED UP FOR PROTECTION.

147

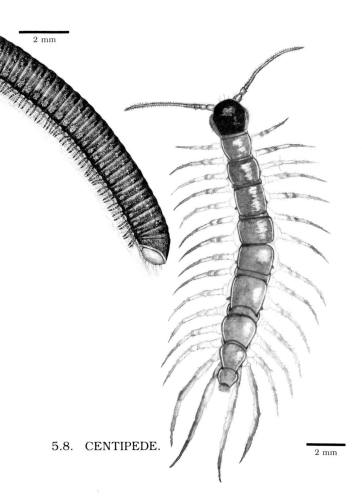

5.7. MILLIPEDE.

With their ungainly number of legs, **millipedes** (Fig. 5.7) and **centipedes** (Fig. 5.8) are often mistaken for each other. Centipedes happen to have one less pair of legs on each body segment and are normally faster than millipedes, but both can have well over 100 pairs of legs.

Whether millipedes and centipedes are slow or fast, they are all graceful. As they glide through the soil or over stones and fallen leaves, all those legs somehow maintain a rhythmic cadence. The neural networks that keep these legs from becoming hopelessly intertwined are an expression of nature's unrivaled design.

Many millipedes and centipedes use chemical repellents to ward off insects and larger predators. They manufacture their own foul-smelling and foul-tasting chemicals in glands that line the sides of their bodies; each gland is lined with an impervious cuticle that protects the animal from it own repellent. If you should disturb a millipede or centipede, you will probably come away with a rather foul-smelling odor on your fingers.

5.8. CENTIPEDE.

148

5.9. DADDY LONGLEGS.

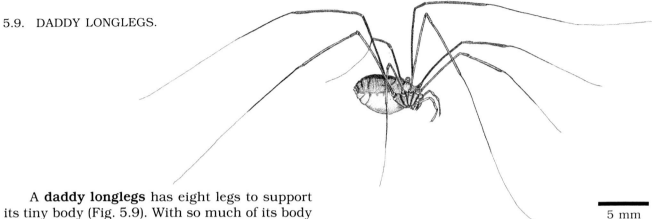

5 mm

A **daddy longlegs** has eight legs to support its tiny body (Fig. 5.9). With so much of its body area devoted to legs, it is not surprising that a daddy longlegs spends a good portion of its time grooming its legs. Notice how meticulously it preens each long leg with its sharp jaws; but despite all this leg grooming, every so often you will see some red soil mites hitching rides aboard these long legs.

The daddy longlegs sometimes loses one or more of its delicate, spindly legs and seems to manage all right unless it loses the second pair of legs. This is the longest pair and the pair that is waved about in traveling over the ground. This flailing of legs was probably the source of an old English belief that these creatures helped farmers with their reaping and that it was bad luck to kill one. The daddy longlegs actually uses its second pair of legs as antennae—for touching and smelling—but the belief probably still lingers in the English countryside and has helped the daddy longlegs earn its other common name—harvestman.

Unlike its relatives the spiders that have eight eyes as well as eight legs, the daddy longlegs only has two eyes, which are perched directly above its second pair of legs.

149

Wolf spiders are not only easy to find among fallen leaves or under boards, but they also make good terrarium pets (Fig. 5.10). One very good and entertaining method for finding wolf spiders is to collect them at night. Head out to a field or your backyard with a flashlight or headlamp and look for the glowing eyes of these spiders. The many fine air tubes (tracheoles) that supply air to each of the spider's eight eyes also act as reflectors for light from your flashlight.

A mother wolf spider is very protective of her silk egg sac and carries it with her wherever she travels. The newly hatched spiders cannot escape from the sac on their own; somehow the mother spider senses their impending hatching and uses her fangs to tear the sac open. As the spiderlings escape, they hop aboard their mother's back and ride about until all the yolk that came packaged in their eggs is depleted. Even if one should fall off while the mother spider goes about her business of hunting, it usually manages to get back on. As soon as a wolf spider hatches, its spinnerets spin out a lifeline that is anchored to the mother spider, and it is this line that leads it back to its brothers and sisters.

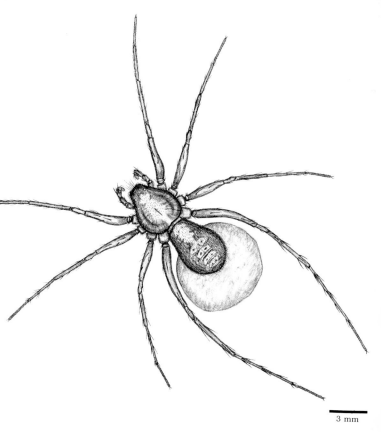

3 mm

5.10. WOLF SPIDER WITH EGG SAC.

150

There are more species of **rove beetles** (Fig. 5.11) than there are species in any other family of beetles, and most of them live in abundance beneath our feet. They are fast moving, and although a few are herbivorous, most are insect eaters.

The short wing covers of rove beetles—one of their distinguishing features—leave most of the abdomen exposed and flexible. If you venture too close to a rove beetle, it will flick up its abdomen as though it is about to sting or spray (Fig. 5.12). It is a good bluff and certainly fools many who intrude on the rove beetle's privacy.

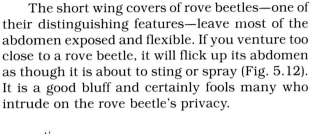

5.11.   ROVE BEETLE.

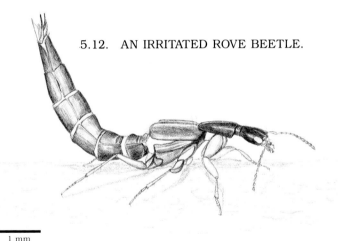

5.12.   AN IRRITATED ROVE BEETLE.

1 mm

2 mm

151

To find the **scarab beetle grub** (Fig. 5.13) and the **cicada nymph** (Fig. 5.14), you will have to dig into the soil where they graze on stands of roots and rootlets. Since both of these insects overwinter beneath the ground, they burrow below the frost line during the colder months of the year and then move up toward the surface with the warmer days of spring. They often spend several years underground, but eventually they forsake their subterranean living for the allure of leaves and flowers. The species of cicada that spends seventeen years underground probably holds the subterranean record.

Few of us ever see a live cicada nymph unless we spend a great deal of time digging holes or ditches, but almost all of us have seen the crunchy shell that each nymph sheds after it crawls aboveground. As its gradual internal transformation from a burrowing nymph to a flying cicada occurs, the nymph begins to ascend from the depths of the soil. When it emerges, it climbs the nearest vertical object where the sudden shedding of its shell will reveal the winged cicada that has formed within. The shell of the nymph is actually its exoskeleton and is a perfect mold of the cicada in its underground form.

152

5.13.   SCARAB BEETLE LARVA (*grub*).

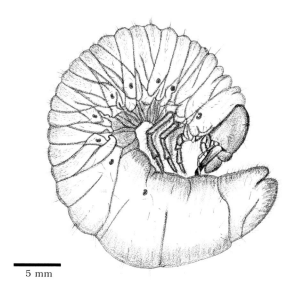

5 mm

5.14. CICADA NYMPH.

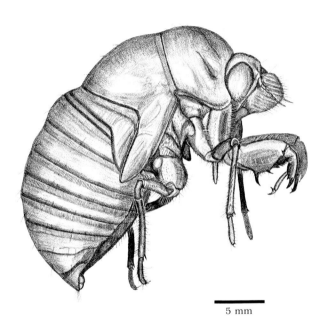

5 mm

The exoskeleton of this formidable-looking creature is brittle but resistant to practically all harsh chemicals, such as acids and bases. Chicken bones will soften enough in even a weak acid such as vinegar that they can be tied in knots, but cicada skeletons do not even begin to dissolve. Soil fungi are one of the few agents that can recycle, in a matter of days, the nutrients bound up in cicada shells.

One would think that underground living would be a fine way to escape predators and parasites. However, the larvae of one family of beetles happen to feed exclusively on cicada nymphs. Scarab beetle grubs face a similar predicament.

153

Pelecinid wasps are elegant-looking insects whose larval days are humbly spent underground as parasites of scarab beetle grubs. With powers of detection that we still do not fully understand, the female wasp always locates the favorite food of her larvae. Even though the beetle grubs usually feed several inches below ground, they are still within range of the female's far-reaching ovipositor (Fig. 5.15).

3 mm

5.15.   FEMALE PELECINID WASP.

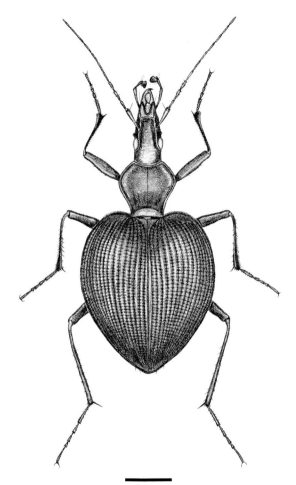

5 mm

5.16. SNAIL-EATING GROUND BEETLE.

A large family of common beetles is known as **ground beetles.** With long legs and sharp jaws, they are well-equipped as predators of the forest floor. Members of this family can be found under logs and stones, in dry or moist soil—in just about every habitat the soil provides. The dark-loving **snail-eating ground beetle** (Fig. 5.16) likes moist, shaded, secluded ravines where it finds its favorite prey, snails.

155

5.17. TIGER BEETLE ADULT.

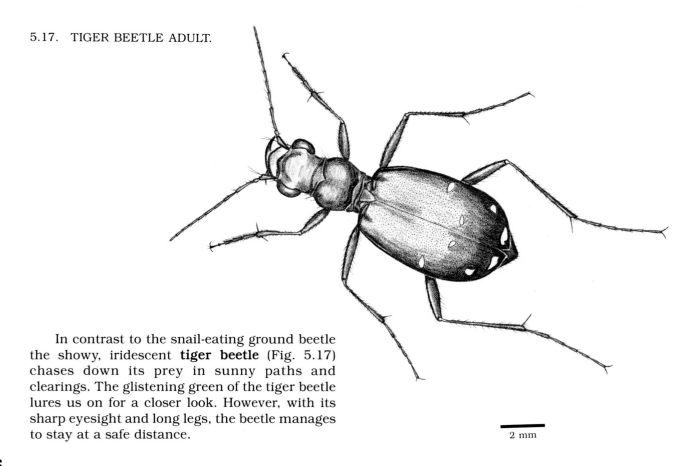

2 mm

In contrast to the snail-eating ground beetle the showy, iridescent **tiger beetle** (Fig. 5.17) chases down its prey in sunny paths and clearings. The glistening green of the tiger beetle lures us on for a closer look. However, with its sharp eyesight and long legs, the beetle manages to stay at a safe distance.

Along the same paths where you find the flashy tiger beetles, there may be groups of tiny pits. At close range you may discover that each pit has a resident whose saberlike jaws block the entrance. Although other small insects cannot fall to the bottom of the pit, they can, and usually do, fall into the jaws of these **tiger beetle larvae** (Fig. 5.18). Insects rarely escape from these jaws since the beetle larva anchors itself to the pit with two sharp hooks located on the hump of its back. These hooks help the larva stand its ground with insects considerably larger than itself. Watch for yourself when you discover a colony of these tiger beetle larvae.

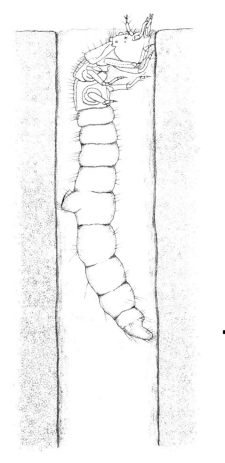

2 mm

5.18.   TIGER BEETLE LARVA IN ITS PIT.

5.19. ANT LION LARVA IN ITS CRATER.

5 mm

Little craters may dot dusty or sandy paths. Although it is not obvious that these craters are inhabited, at the bottom of each lies the larva of an **ant lion** waiting for some creature, often an ant, to tumble over the rim of its crater (Fig. 5.19). The sides of the crater are so steep and crumbly that once an insect or spider has wandered over the edge, it usually tumbles into the jaws of the larva. Sometimes the victim's descent into the crater is assisted by the larva; with a quick flip of its flat head, the larva tosses a few grains of sand at the victim. If you ever catch the ant lion in the act of digging a crater, you will see how it literally uses its head to pitch sand from the hole.

The ant lion larva (Fig. 5.20) looks like an enlarged version of the aphid lion and it feeds with the same type of jaws (p. 84). The adult looks like a damselfly with long antennae but is more closely related to the lacewing (p. 85). In fact, all of them—ant lion, aphid lion, and lacewing—are members of the same insect order, Neuroptera (*neuron,* nerve; *ptera,* wings).

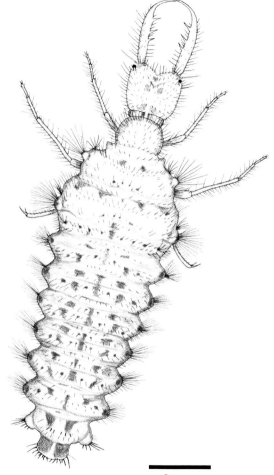

5.20.   ANT LION LARVA.

2 mm

159

Ants and their colonies can be found in large numbers almost everywhere beneath our feet. Professor E. O. Wilson, an authority on ants as well as many other biological subjects, recently described the awesome sizes of some ant colonies. He told of one "super-city" on the Japanese island of Hokkaido reported to have over 1 million queens and over 300 million workers. Most of the ant colonies that we find can be considered towns in comparison to this super-city. The ants of a particular colony usually have only a single queen who is the mother of all the workers, which are all females (Fig. 5.21). While their mother continues laying more and more eggs, workers cooperate in tending the eggs, feeding and cleaning their younger sisters as well as foraging above ground for food (Fig. 5.22).

Some worker ants, however, are incapable of even the simplest housekeeping chores; they survive only by pillaging worker pupae from colonies of other ant species. These "slaves" perform all the necessary chores in their new colony and tend the young of the slave-making queen as though they were their own sisters.

Once a year the routine of every colony usually is broken when winged ants develop from

5.21. WORKER ANT.

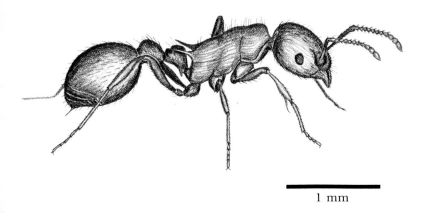

1 mm

160

5.22. WORKER ANTS TENDING EGGS.

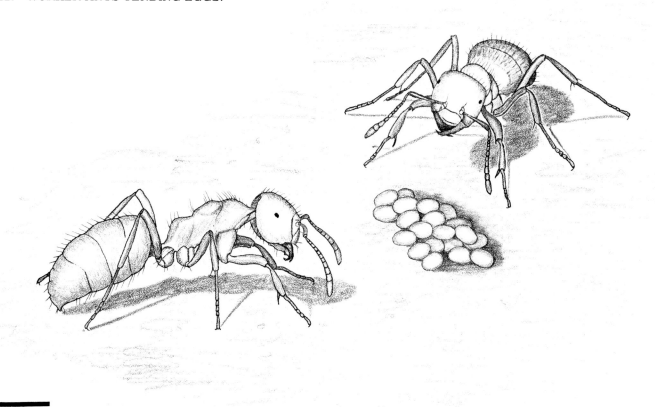

1 mm

the eggs laid by the old queen. These are males and new queens that swarm forth from the colony to mate. Clouds of flying and mating ants are sometimes common in the spring. The smaller males die soon after this aerial adventure, but the larger queens bite off their wings and settle down to start new colonies beneath the ground.

You can keep a whole colony of ants in a large, widemouthed jar but be careful about your choice of ants; a few species are known to have very irritating bites and stings. After you have found ants that neither bite nor sting, carefully scoop them out with a spade and place the soil and the ants on newspaper. Almost fill the jar with loose soil and then, with a spoon, add ants of all ages to the jar (Fig. 5.23). If you are lucky, you will add the queen, but even without the queen the workers will rear the young and maintain the colony for many weeks. Cap the jar with a piece of cloth and a rubber band. After the ants have settled in and have constructed their cham-

bers and passageways, add pieces of fruit, bread, a little sugar, and some water. Replace these items with fresh food if mold starts to appear.

Watch how ants "sniff out" trails with their antennae. Ants, like female moths and termites,

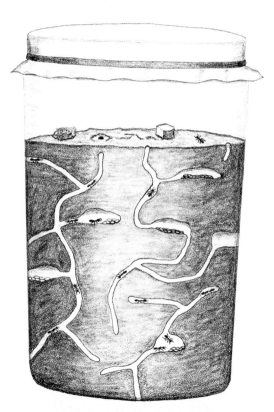

5.23.   ANT COLONY IN A JAR.

leave trails of chemicals called pheromones that other members of their colony follow. It is a good way to navigate in the underground corridors.

By keeping the ants in a cool, dark spot when you are not watching, they should prosper for several weeks. After you have enjoyed watching them, return the ants to the spot where you found them.

CLASSIFICATION

Class Arachnida
    Spiders
        Order Araneida (*aranea*, spider)
            Family Lycosidae (*lycos*, wolf): **wolf spider**

    Mites
        Order Acarina (*acarus*, mite)
            Family Trombidiidae (*trombid*, little timid one): **red velvet mite**

    Daddy longlegs (Harvestmen)
        Order Opiliones (*opilio*, shepherd)
            Family Phalangiidae (*phalangium*, a kind of spider): **daddy longlegs**

Class Crustacea
    Isopods
        Order Isopoda (*isos*, equal; *poda*, feet)
            Family Porcellionidae (*porca*, sow; *-ellus*, little): **sow bug**
            Family Armadillidiidae (*armadillo* [Spanish], armorlike coat: *-idus*, similar to): **pill bug**

Class Insecta
    Springtails
        Order Collembola (*colla*, glue; *embolos*, peg)
            Family Entomobryidae (*entomon*, insect; *bryum*, moss): **springtail**

Aphids, Cicadas, Hoppers, Psyllids, Spittle Bugs
    Order Homoptera (*homos*, same; *ptera*, wings)
        Family Cicadidae (*cicada*, a cicada): **cicada** nymph

Dobson Flies, Lacewings, Ant Lions
    Order Neuroptera (*neuron*, nerve; *ptera*, wings)
        Family Myrmeleontidae (*myrmex*, ant; *leo*, lion): **ant lion** larva

Beetles
    Order Coleoptera (*coleos*, sheath; *ptera*, wings)
        Family Staphylinidae (*staphylinos*, a kind of beetle): **rove beetles**
        Family Scarabaeidae (*scarabaeus*, a kind of beetle): **scarab beetle** larva (grub)
        Family Cicindelidae (*cicindela*, a kind of beetle): **tiger beetle** adult and larva
        Family Carabidae (*carabus*, a kind of beetle): **snail-eating ground beetle**

Ants, Bees, Wasps
    Order Hymenoptera (*hymen*, membrane; *ptera*, wings)
        Family Pelecinidae (*pelecion*, little ax): **pelecinid wasp**
        Family Formicidae (*formica*, ant): **ants**

Class Myriapoda
    Stone Centipedes
        Order Lithobiomorpha (*lithos*, stone; *bios*, life; *morphe*, form)
            Family Lithobiidae (*lithos*, stone; *bios*, life): **stone centipede**

Millipedes
    Order Iulida (*iulus*, millipede)
        Family Iulidae (*iulus*, millipede): **millipede**

ADDITIONAL READING

INSECTS, spiders, and their relatives are so diverse that no one book can possibly provide more than a small sampling of the kaleidoscope of arthropod life. Scientists continue to discover new species of arthropods, and our understanding of how and why these animals carry on their affairs is steadily growing.

The field guides that are available are not only useful for identification but also contain many interesting anecdotes on insects and their relatives. All these guides are filled with attractive and accurate illustrations. The Audubon Society field guide has over 700 color photographs of spiders and insects.

Milne, L., and M. Milne. 1980. *The Audubon Society Field Guide to North American Insects and Spiders.* New York: Alfred A. Knopf, 989 pp.

Books in the Peterson Field Guide Series, such as the one by Borror and White, are known for their detailed illustrations with arrows pointing to important distinguishing features.

Borror, D. J., and R. E. White. 1970. *A Field Guide to the Insects.* Boston: Houghton Mifflin Co., 404 pp.

The two old stand-bys by Lutz and Swain have continued to maintain their appeal to naturalists for several decades.

Lutz, F. E. 1935. *Field Book of Insects.* New York: G. P. Putnam Sons, 510 pp.
Swain, R. B. 1948. *The Insect Guide.* Garden City, N.Y.: Doubleday, 261 pp.

The last two guides that are listed are books

in the series of Golden Nature Guides, which is known for its accuracy, conciseness, and simplicity.

Levi, H. W., and L. R. Levi. 1968. *Spiders and Their Kin.* New York: Golden Press, 160 pp.

Zim, H. S., and C. Cottam. 1956. *Insects: A Guide to Familiar American Insects.* New York: Simon and Schuster, 160 pp.

Other books provide detailed information on just a few species from the broad spectrum of insect and spider life.

Howard Evans has had a lifelong fascination with insects and has written both scholarly articles and popular books about them. In *Wasp Farm,* he tells about the wasps that lived on his small farm near Ithaca, New York. In *Life on a Little-known Planet* and *The Pleasures of Entomology,* he draws on scientific articles as well as personal experience in writing about the lives of a few familiar insects.

Evans, H. E. 1963. *Wasp Farm.* New York: Natural History Press, 178 pp.

_____. 1978. *Life on a Little-known Planet.* New York: E. P. Dutton, 318 pp.

_____. 1985. *The Pleasures of Entomology.* Washington, D.C.: Smithsonian Institution Press, 238 pp.

During the last thirty years of his life, Jean Henri Fabre observed and chronicled the lives of insects and spiders on his small farm in southern France. This beautifully illustrated book contains excerpts from his many writings.

Fabre, J. H. 1979. *Insects,* ed. David Black. New York: Charles Scribner Sons, 108 pp.

Time-Life books are known for the clarity of their texts and the attractiveness of their illustrations. This volume is no exception.

Farb, P., and editors of Life. 1962. *The Insects.* Life Nature Library. New York: Time, Inc, 192 pp.

In the third volume of *The Animal Kingdom,* John Pallister discusses the natural history of all the major groups of arthropods. His account mixes interesting tales with accurate scientific information.

Pallister, J. C. 1954. "Animals with Jointed Legs." In *The Animal Kingdom*, Vol. 3, ed. Frederick Drimmer. New York: Greystone Press, 298 pp.

These two wildlife photographers have written a detailed book on all aspects of spider life and have filled it with outstanding color photographs.

Preston-Mafham, R., and K. Preston-Mafham. 1984. *Spiders of the World.* New York: Facts on File, Inc., 191 pp.

This guide to insects acquaints readers not only with the intriguing ways of sixty common insects but also helps readers find these insects on their own.

Stokes, D. W. 1983. *A Guide to Observing Insect Lives.* Boston: Little, Brown and Co., 371 pp.

These well-known nature writers tell about fourteen common insects in this book for young readers. Handsome, detailed drawings by D. D. Tyler accompany the text.

Graham, A., and F. Graham. 1983. *Busy Bugs.* New York: Dodd, Mead & Co., 63 pp.

This book is a good introduction to insects and activities with insects for younger children. The author is not only a renowned biologist but also is a host of a Canadian Broadcasting Corporation series on nature.

Suzuki, D. 1986. *Looking at Insects.* Toronto: Stoddart Publishing Co., 96 pp.

Helen Ross Russell has written extensively about nature study. In this small book for young children, she calls our attention to the small worlds that are about us everywhere and the little creatures that inhabit them. Many close-up photographs add to the book's appeal.

Russell, H. R. 1972. *Small Worlds.* Boston: Little, Brown and Co., 32 pp.

Edwin Way Teale was a naturalist who began his career writing about the lives of the insects and spiders in his backyard. He was also an accomplished photographer, and his books contain many close-up views of these creatures.

Teale, E. W. 1937. *Grassroot Jungles.* New York: Dodd, Mead & Co., 233 pp.
_____. 1939. *The Boys' Book of Insects.* New York: E. P. Dutton, 237 pp.
_____. 1962. *The Strange Lives of Familiar Insects.* New York: Dodd, Mead & Co., 208 pp.

Sir Vincent Wigglesworth has spent a distinguished career at Cambridge University studying the lives of insects. With the help of many drawings and photographs, he describes what he and other scientists have learned about the ways of insects.

Wigglesworth, V. B. 1964. *The Life of Insects.* New York: The World Publishing Co., 360 pp.

Amateur entomologists will find a wealth of information on insect life in this book written by two professional entomologists.

Arnett, R. H., and R. L. Jacques. 1985. *Insect Life: A Field Entomology Manual for the Amateur Naturalist.* Englewood Cliffs, N.J.: Prentice-Hall, Inc., 354 pp.

APPENDIX
Suppliers and Their Supplies

AT SOME TIMES of the year you might not be able to find certain arthropods outdoors. Raising a butterfly or listening to cricket music are just two activities with arthropods that can brighten the weeks of winter. Three supply houses offer a large, year-round selection of arthropods and helpful information on keeping these arthropods at home or at school. These supply houses are also good sources for magnifying lenses and stereomicroscopes.

Carolina Biological Supply Company
East Coast address
2700 York Road
Burlington, North Carolina 27215

West Coast address
P.O. Box 187
Gladstone, Oregon 97027

Ask for their free *Carolina Arthropods Manual.*

Animals Available

Ants and ant nests	Flour beetles
Bees and observation hives	Hornworms
	Ladybird beetles
Bess beetles	Milkweed bugs
Butterflies	Millipedes
Caterpillars	Moth cocoons
Centipedes	Parasitic wasps
Cockroaches	Praying mantises
Crickets	Spiders
Damselfly nymphs	Termites
Dragonfly nymphs	Various crustaceans of ponds and streams
Earwigs	
Flies	Wood lice

Ward's Natural Science Establishment, Inc.
East Coast address
5100 West Henrietta Road
P.O. Box 92912
Rochester, New York 14692

West Coast address
11850 East Florence Avenue
Santa Fe Springs, California 90670

Animals Available
Ants and ant nests
Bees and observation
hives
Butterflies
Caterpillars
Cockroaches
Crickets
Flies

Isopods, amphipods, and
other crustaceans of
ponds and streams
Milkweed bugs
Praying mantis egg cases
Termites
Wood lice

Connecticut Valley Biological Supply Co., Inc.
82 Valley Road
P.O. Box 326
Southampton, Massachusetts 01073

Animals Available
Amphipods
Ants and ant nests
Bees and observation
hives
Caddis fly larvae
Cockroaches
Crickets
Damselfly nymphs
Dragonfly nymphs

Fairy shrimp
Flour beetles
Fruit flies
Isopods
Ladybird beetles
Mayfly nymphs
Milkweed bugs
Moth cocoons
Termites

170

INDEX

175

176

177

183